WILLIAM CAREY

Father of Modern Missions

WILLIAM CAREY

Father of
Modern Missions

by

Walter Bruce Davis

MOODY PRESS
CHICAGO

*To Mr. Robert D. Clark of Edinburgh,
Scotland, through whose generous help
I trained as a missionary.*

Contents

Chapter One—Early Life and
               Missionary Call 7

Chapter Two—Early Missionary Work
               in Bengal 32

Chapter Three—Serampore, 1800-1813 48

Chapter Four—Serampore, 1814-1834. 74

Appendix A—The Serampore Form of
               Agreement 109

Appendix B—Charter of Incorporation
               of Serampore College. 129

Appendix C—Statutes and Regulations
               of Serampore College. 137

Appendix D—Article VI, Clause 2, of
               the Treaty of Purchase,
               Transferring Serampore
               to the British Govern-
               ment 143

Bibliography 144

5

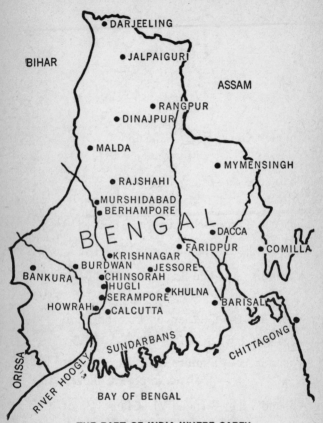

**THE PART OF INDIA WHERE CAREY
LABORED, SHOWING PRINCIPAL MISSION STATIONS**
(Some of this area now constitutes East Pakistan)

Chapter One

Early Life and Missionary Call

WILLIAM CAREY was born on August 17, 1761 to Edmund Carey, a poor handloom weaver, and his wife Elizabeth in a humble thatched cottage in the village of Paulerspury, Northamptonshire, England. He was born during the reign of George III, an age described as very pleasant to live in [1] and in eventful times. At home, England was experiencing a quickening of spiritual and religious life through the revivals of John Wesley. Overseas, England was entering the final stages of the Seven Years' War (1756-1763), which brought about English supremacy in India and Canada.

---

[1] Robinson, England: *A History of British Progress,* p. 444.

Carey's early childhood, though spent in the midst of poverty, was not unhappy, for the cottage in which he lived was situated in the midst of lovely countryside, and his God-fearing parents sought to make life meaningful and pleasant for him. When Carey was six, his father was appointed to the dual office of village schoolmaster and parish clerk in the St. James' Anglican Church of Paulerspury. The family took up residence in the schoolhouse, and their interests now centered around the village school and the church. In the former, Carey received the only formal education he was ever to have, and in the latter, where he served as choirboy, he was confirmed an Anglican.

Carey was a precocious child. He read avidly all the books he was able to obtain, including a Latin grammar and dictionary, many of whose words he memorized. He early displayed a thirst for knowledge about plants, and acquired an amazing amount of information about them.

Carey's schooling came to an end in 1775 when he was fourteen, and his future employment had then to be decided. He was short, heavyset, and strong, and would have done well on a farm had he not suffered from a skin allergy which outdoor work aggravated. It is interesting that his father did not have him trained in his own trade of weaving, but decided to apprentice him to Clarke Nichols, a shoemaker of Piddington, eight miles from Paulerspury. It may be that Carey's parents were already aware that his hands lacked the deftness needed by a good weaver, and had assumed it took less cleverness of hands to be a shoemaker than a weaver.

As an apprentice in shoe-repairing and shoemaking, Carey stayed in Nichols' home, where he and his fellow apprentice, John Warr, were subject to the rough discipline of their master, who had a vile temper and engaged in frequent drinking bouts. Carey soon discovered that Nichols possessed a small library and that one of the books in it was a New Testament commentary which contained Greek words and phrases. Carey was fascinated by Greek and immediately took up the study of the language in his spare time.

The worldly atmosphere of Nichols' home began to influence Carey's manner of life, and gradually he lost interest in maintaining the moral and spiritual standards which his parents had taught him. This change in Carey greatly disturbed Warr, who had recently been converted and who now made every effort to bring about Carey's conversion. Warr was an ardent Nonconformist and was constantly urging Carey to leave the Anglican fold and enter that of Nonconformity. It was difficult for

Carey to resist the importunacy of one so close
to him, so he finally agreed to attend the Nonconformist prayer meeting at nearby Hackleton. Here Carey heard clearly explained the
need for sinners personally to trust in the Lord
Jesus Christ as the Saviour from sin and openly
confess Him before others. He did not feel
ready to reach any decision at this time, but he
faithfully attended both Anglican and Nonconformist services. A few months before his
eighteenth birthday, Carey made public profession of his faith in Christ. Some months
later, in February, 1779, he made another momentous decision, namely, to become a Nonconformist. This was a difficult step for Carey
to take because he knew it would greatly distress his parents, who were zealous Anglicans.

With characteristic enthusiasm, Carey began earnestly to develop his newfound faith in
Christ. He faithfully studied the Bible; he read
widely in religious books which he borrowed
from friends; he engaged in religious discussions with Anglican and Nonconformist think-
ers in the neighborhood; he accepted opportunities to preach; and he successfully sought
the conversion of others including his master,
Nichols, who repented on his deathbed.

In 1779, upon the death of Nichols, Carey
became the employee of another shoemaker,
Thomas Old of Hackleton. Two years later,

when barely twenty, Carey married twenty-five-year-old Dorothy Plackett, his master's sister-in-law, who could neither read nor write. It seems surprising that Carey, who reveled in books, in the acquisition of knowledge, and in the acquiring of languages, should marry an illiterate woman who had not the faintest interest in such things, nor the slightest desire to become interested. Concerning this marriage, J. C. Marshman states:

> This imprudent union proved a severe clog on his exertions for more than twenty-five years. His illiterate wife, who possessed no feeling in unison with his own, was altogether unsuited for his companionship; and the great tenderness which always marked his conduct towards her, places the meekness and nobleness of his character in a strong light.[2]

George Smith writes of Carey's marriage to Dorothy Plackett:

> Never had minister, missionary, or scholar a less sympathetic mate, due largely to the latent mental disease which in India carried her off; but for more than twenty years the husband showed her loving reverence.[3]

[2] Marshman, *The Life and Labours of Carey, Marshman and Ward*, pp. 4, 5.
[3] Smith, *The Life of William Carey. D.D.*, p. 23.

Troubles in Carey's life began to multiply. His first-born child, Ann, died from fever; a prolonged attack of fever endangered his own life and left him bald; his employer, Old, died suddenly in 1783 and left him with serious business problems; and his earnings became so meager that he found it difficult to make ends meet. Carey was, however, possessed with an obduracy which enabled him doggedly to make progress, however great the difficulties which beset him. He continued faithfully to serve the churches at Earls Barton and Pury End as lay pastor even though the remuneration barely covered his expenses; he opened a fee-paying school in the village to augment his income, even though he much disliked teaching children; [4] and he undertook the acquiring of yet another language, Hebrew, and the reading of still more books, even though he had less time at his disposal for study than formerly because of the evening school.

It was during these years of hardship that Carey's mind became preoccupied with the condition of the heathen and the evangelization of the world. Three books influenced Carey's thinking about missions: the Bible, which clearly taught him that it is the Church's duty to preach the Gospel to every creature;

---

[4] Marshman, *The Life and Labours of Carey, Marshman and Ward*, p. 5.

the life of David Brainerd, which amply demonstrated the effectiveness of missions when engaged in by a dedicated missionary; and *Captain Cook's Voyages,* whose vivid portrayal of moral and spiritual conditions in the South Sea Islands made clear the crying need for missions. From this time Carey prayed regularly for the heathen.

Carey had also been giving much thought to the question of the teaching of Baptists respecting believers' baptism. Upon becoming a Nonconformist, he had joined the Congregational Church. But from time to time he came into contact with Baptists, who explained to him their doctrine of baptism and the Church. In October, 1783, after careful consideration of the issues involved, Carey requested believers' baptism and was baptized by immersion in the River Nene at Northampton by John Ryland, a Baptist minister.

In 1785, learning that the schoolmaster of the nearby parish of Moulton had closed his school and moved elsewhere, Carey decided to settle in Moulton, open a school, and also carry on his trade of shoemaking. In keeping with the law of those days respecting all those whose annual rent was under £ 10, Carey had to furnish a certificate to the overseers of the Moulton Parish from the overseers of the Paulerspury Parish stating that the Parish of Paulerspury would be responsible for him and his family if they became paupers.

Since Carey's school was the only one in the parish, it soon had a good enrollment, and Carey's income was satisfactory. The former schoolmaster, however, unexpectedly returned, reopened his school, and regained many of his pupils who had enrolled in Carey's school, thus drastically reducing Carey's earnings from teaching.

Carey found that the Baptist church in Moulton was in a pitiful state. The church had been without a minister for several years, and its spiritual condition was at a low ebb; the members had become so lax about church attendance that services were held only on rare occasions; and the church building was badly in need of repairs. Carey was given an opportunity to remedy this state of affairs, for Moulton Baptists invited him to become their lay pastor. He accepted, and entered this new sphere of service with much enthusiasm. His zealous labor was richly blessed of God, for the church entered upon times of genuine revival. The secret of Carey's success as a minister was not distinguished preaching (judged by standards of homiletics and oratory). In fact, the Olny Baptist church, of which Carey had become a member and to which he applied in 1785 for ordination to the ministry, refused his petition after hearing him preach and told him to make application after he had gained more experience in preaching. It must, however, be gratefully recognized that though Carey's sermons lacked style and finish, he preached them with such sincerity and passion that sinners were convicted and converted. The Olny church later acknowledged Carey's call to the ministry and recommended his ordination, which took place in Moulton in August, 1787.

The fact that Carey was now an ordained Baptist minister undoubtedly enhanced his status as pastor of the Moulton Baptist church, but unfortunately it did not increase his stipend, which remained at £10 annually, supplemented by an annual grant of £5 from the London Particular Baptist Fund, an income quite insufficient to maintain Carey and his family. To keep up his income, he had to continue cobbling and teaching school. In the meantime, Carey had taken up the study of two other languages, French and Dutch. When his employer in the shoe trade, Mr. Gotch, learned that Carey read regularly in Latin, Greek, Hebrew, French, and Dutch, he was so amazed and so pleased that he insisted upon giving Carey a weekly sum of 10/—(at that time approximately $2.50) in order that Carey could give up shoemaking and devote more time to study.

In the midst of his busy life, Carey continued to pray regularly for the heathen about whose spiritual condition he was becoming more and more concerned. He was much disturbed to find that few of his colleagues in the ministry shared this concern. At a meeting of the Ministers' Fraternal of the Northampton Association when Carey suggested as a topic, "Whether the Command given to the Apostles to teach all nations was not binding on all succeeding ministers to the end of the world seeing that the accompanying promise was of equal extent," he was told by the senior Ryland, "Young man, sit down, sit down. When God pleases to convert the heathen, He'll do it without consulting you or me." Carey was so troubled by this heartless response and the generally indifferent attitude of his fellow ministers that he felt compelled to express his missionary convictions in pamphlet form and thus reach a wider and perhaps more responsive group.

The pamphlet was eventually published in 1792 under the title "An Enquiry into the Obligations of Christians to use means for the Conversion of the Heathens, in which the Religious State of the Different Nations of the World, the success of Former undertakings, and the practicability of further undertakings are considered, by William Carey." The main points made by Carey in the "Enquiry" are as follows: the population of the world is approximately 731 millions, of whom 557 millions are non-Christians; the deplorable moral and spiritual condition of the heathen is a call to Christian action; the Great Commission is still binding upon Christ's followers; each of the chief problems which faces every prospective missionary—the danger of living among barbarians, the difficulty of securing supplies, the herculean task of learning the languages—can and should be resolutely overcome; and a society should be organized to promote home and foreign missions. George Smith, a biographer of Carey, considered Carey's "Enquiry" in 1885 to be the "first and still greatest missionary treatise in the English language." [5]

Carey's ability as a pastor, especially in dealing with troublesome situations in the life of the church, was becoming known throughout the Association.

In Leicester the Harvey Lane Baptist church, which had been passing through a crucial period because of moral lapses on the part of members, felt that Carey was the one who could best help to restore the church to

[5] Smith, *The Life of William Carey, D.D.,* p. 40.

purity and vitality, and in 1789 invited him to
be pastor. Carey accepted the call with high
hopes, and for some months the church made
excellent progress under his leadership, but
quarrels broke out once again among members, and the spiritual life of the congregation
sank to a low ebb. Conditions did not improve
until the church, at Carey's suggestion, voted
to dissolve. It then reorganized itself on the
basis of a new constitution which contained so
strict a discipline that it was quite unacceptable to members who had been unruly, and by
this strategy such members were excluded. The
consequent reduction in membership, while
achieving harmony, had financial repercussions. The smaller congregation was unable to
give their pastor enough salary to cover the
living expenses of himself, his wife and three
sons. Carey had, therefore, to engage in teaching and shoemaking to subsist in Leicester.
Yet, amazingly enough this minister-shoe-
maker-teacher also found time to read widely
in theology, languages, literature, and science,
to make his services freely available to pastor-
less village churches in the Leicester area, and
to act as secretary of the Leicester Nonconformist Committee which championed the
cause of Nonconformity.

Increasingly the burden of the Church's missionary responsibility weighed heavily upon

Carey's soul, and he availed himself of every opportunity to express this concern to others. He was gratified to be associated with three colleagues in the Northampton Association, John Ryland, John Sutcliff, and Andrew Fuller who shared in large measure his solicitude for the heathen. The first two had been instrumental in organizing in 1784 a prayer movement which for an hour on the first Monday of every month prayed, among other things, for "the spread of the Gospel in the most distant parts of the habitable globe," and the last-named through his sermons and his writings attacked the lifeless theology of the Baptist church of his day which held that the Gospel is meant only for the elect and which, therefore, opposed missions to the heathen.

In 1791, at Clipston, where the Northamptonshire Baptist Association met, Sutcliff and Fuller preached sermons which were warmly missionary, and Carey urged the association to form then and there a society to propagate the Gospel among the heathen. But the members of the association declined on the grounds that they had neither the ability nor the resources for such a venture. The following year the association met at Nottingham, and on the second day, May 31, Carey preached a simple yet dynamic missionary sermon based on the text Isaiah 54:2-3:

Enlarge the place of thy tent, and let them
stretch forth the curtains of thine habitations:
spare not, lengthen thy cords, and strengthen
thy stakes; for thou shalt break forth on the
right hand and on the left; and thy seed shall
inherit the Gentiles, and make the desolate
cities to be inhabited.

It was in this sermon that Carey enunciated
the principles which he felt should character-
ize the missionary movement: "Expect great
things from God, attempt great things for
God."

Carey's deeply moving words so impressed
the association delegates that after some dis-
cussion they adopted the following resolution:

Resolved, that a plan be prepared against the
next Ministers' Meeting at Kettering for
forming a Baptist Society for propagating the
Gospel among the Heathens.

Carey was jubilant that the association had
made this momentous decision, and he began
carefully to formulate plans for a missionary
society to present to his fellow ministers when
next they met in formal session. The ministers'
meeting was held at Kettering on October 2,
1792. At the evening session, which convened
in the back parlor of the home of a hospitable
Baptist widow, Mrs. Beeby Wallis, there were
present twelve Baptist ministers: William

Carey, Andrew Fuller, John Ryland, John Sutcliff, Reynold Hogg, Abraham Greenwood, Edward Sherman, Samuel Pearce, Joshua Burton, Thomas Blundel, William Heighton and John Ayres; a Baptist deacon, Joseph Timms; and a Baptist divinity student, William Staughton, who later went to the U. S. A. and became prominent in American Baptist foreign mission affairs. These are the men who under the guidance of the Spirit of God organized the first Protestant missionary society to have an ecumenical vision, for the avowed object of the society was the preaching of the Gospel "to every creature."

The following resolutions were adopted at Kettering:

1. Desirous of making an effort for the propagation of the Gospel among the heathen, agreeably to what is recommended in brother Carey's late publication on that subject, we, whose names appear to the subsequent subscription, do solemnly agree to act in society together for that purpose.

2. As in the present divided state of Christendom, it seems that each denomination, by exerting itself separately, is most likely to accomplish the great ends of a mission, it is agreed that this society be called "The

Particular Baptist Society for Propagating the Gospel among the Heathen."

3. As such an undertaking must needs be attended with expense, we agree immediately to open a subscription for the above purpose, and to recommend it to others.

4. Every person who shall subscribe £10 at once, or ten shillings and sixpence annually, shall be considered a member of the society.

5. That the Rev. John Ryland, Reynold Hogg, William Carey, John Sutcliff, and Andrew Fuller, be appointed a committee, three of whom shall be empowered to act in carrying into effect the purposes of this society.

6. That the Rev. Reynold Hogg be appointed treasurer, and the Rev. Andrew Fuller, secretary.

7. That the subscriptions be paid in at the Northampton Ministers' Meeting, October 31, 1792, at which time the subject shall be considered more particularly by the committee and other subscribers who may be present.

Signed, John Ryland, Reynold Hogg, John Sutcliff, Andrew Fuller, Abraham Greenwood, Edward Sherman, Joshua Burton, William Heighton, John Eayres, Joseph Timms: whose subscriptions in all amounted to £13: 2: 6. (at the time approximately $64.25).

The formation of this missionary society on

October 2, 1792, a society described by Dr. George Smith as "the first purely English Missionary Society, which sent forth its own English founder," [6] is generally considered to be the birth of the modern missionary movement. Even those who hold the genesis of modern missions to have been before 1792 recognize and acknowledge the great significance of the Kettering resolutions. Latourette, for example, writes:

> The organization of the Baptist Missionary Society is usually called the inception of the modern Protestant foreign missionary enterprise. In one sense this is not in accord with the facts. As we saw in the preceding volume, more than two centuries before Carey Protestants had had missions among non-Christians, and the eighteenth century had been marked by a rising tide of Protestant efforts in many parts of the world to win pagans to the Christian faith. Yet in another sense Carey marks the beginning of a new era. He seems to have been the first Anglo-Saxon Protestant either in America or Great Britain to propose that Christians take concrete steps to bring their Gospel to all the human race . . . William Carey and the society which arose in response to his faith were in fact the beginning of an

---

[6] *Ibid.*, p. 51.

astounding series of Protestant efforts to reach the entire world with the Christian message.[7]

When Baptists throughout the British Isles first learned the surprising news that their brethren in Northamptonshire had organized a foreign missionary society, they did not display much enthusiasm for the new project. A few churches and individuals made generous contributions, but the London ministers, who represented the most influential Baptist Association in England, were sceptical and held aloof. None of this discouraged Carey, who was already busily engaged in the task of persuading his fellow ministers to send him either to Tahiti or West Africa as the first missionary of the newly founded society.

Meanwhile, Carey received a letter from Dr. John Thomas, a medical doctor who had recently returned from Bengal for the avowed purpose of arousing interest in Bengal as a mission field and who expressed hope that the new Society might give him sufficient financial aid to enable him to return to Bengal as a missionary. Carey proposed to his colleagues that the missionary committee invite Thomas to meet them and talk things over. In the meantime, Andrew Fuller, the committee secretary, made inquiries concerning Thomas and se-

---

[7] Latourette, *A History of the Expansion of Christianity*, Volume IV, pp. 68, 69.

cured the following information about him:
Thomas was a Baptist who had been trained in
medicine and had served several years as a
ship's doctor, first in the British Navy, then
with the East India Company. But his great
interest in the souls as well as the bodies of
men had led Thomas, on one of his voyages to
India, to settle in Bengal among the natives for
three years during which time, financially supported by Christian friends in the East India
Company, he had learned the Bengali language, translated some of the New Testament
into Bengali, and engaged in medical and missionary work.

The formal meeting with Thomas took place
in Kettering on January 9, 1793, and the committee listened with great interest as he told
some of his missionary experiences, and presented a report full of optimism concerning
the possibilities of missionary work in Bengal.
On the basis of this report, the committee appointed Thomas and Carey as the first missionaries of the society with Bengal as their
field of service.

The wisdom of the committee in appoint-
ing Thomas on such slight acquaintance has
been questioned, for it soon became apparent,
after his appointment as a missionary, that he
was eccentric, erratic, changeable, overopti-
mistic, lacking in sound judgment, and im-

provident. But it must gratefully be acknowledged that Thomas, in spite of his failings, rendered Carey and the committee great service by putting their plans for foreign missionary work into actual operation, and doing so in India, a land which offered tremendous scope for Carey's genius in languages.

Carey's decision to go to Bengal as a missionary was made joyously and enthusiastically in the firm conviction that this was God's will for him, but he soon discovered that this view was not shared by his father, who was sure that his son had completely gone out of his mind, nor by his wife, who positively refused to have anything whatsoever to do with the scheme. These reactions greatly distressed Carey, but they did not in any way alter his decision. He was able, however, to reach an agreement with his wife whereby he would take the eldest son Felix with him to Bengal and return for his wife and the rest of the family when the mission was firmly established in Bengal.

Two difficult tasks faced the committee following the decision to send Carey and Thomas to India: the raising of funds sufficient to cover the missionaries' passage money and their living expenses in India for the first year, and the obtaining, for the missionaries, of the East India Company license required of all persons who wished to reside in the company's terri-

tories, and without which the missionaries
would not be able to sail to Bengal in any English ship nor to settle in Bengal. The first task,
that of raising money, was undertaken by Andrew Fuller, the committee secretary, and
proved arduous. The second task, that of securing licenses, ended in complete failure. The
application requesting permission for two missionaries to reside in Bengal was made at an
inopportune time, for the East India Company
had just defeated a resolution being considered
by Parliament which would have required the
company to send missionaries and teachers to
India at company expense, a proposal wholly
unacceptable to the company directors, who
had little interest in the moral and spiritual
welfare of the natives in territories under their
control. So the company, being more touchy
than usual on the question of missionaries,
flatly refused to grant licenses to Carey and
Thomas.

This apparently insuperable problem, however, appeared to be partially solved when
Captain White of the "Earl of Oxford," in
which ship Thomas had previously been surgeon, agreed to take them to India without
East India Company licenses.

Since there was a definite sailing in view, the
committee decided to arrange a valedictory
service for Carey and Thomas. This was held

in Leicester on March 20, 1793 in the presence of a large congregation. A few days later, Carey and his eight-year-old son Felix left home for London, where on April 4 they and the Thomas party consisting of Dr. and Mrs. Thomas, their daughter Betsey, and two cousins, embarked on the "Earl of Oxford." The ship sailed to Portsmouth and anchored in the river for six weeks, waiting for the convoy. Shortly before the convoy was due to sail, Captain White received an anonymous note warning him that his action in taking unlicensed persons as passengers was known in London, and if he persisted in this he stood in danger of losing his command. The letter was probably written by one of Thomas' creditors who had discovered that Thomas was leaving the country without making satisfactory arrangements for the payment of his debts. Captain White ordered Carey and Thomas to leave the ship immediately, but he agreed to permit Mrs. Thomas, Betsey, and the cousins to make the voyage to India.

It was with deep dismay that Carey, Thomas, and Felix watched the "Oxford" sail without them. As they discussed their next step, Thomas, with characteristic resourcefulness, proposed that they store their baggage in Portsmouth and journey without delay to London to inquire if passages could be secured on any foreign vessel sailing to India, for it was obvious that their chances of sailing on any English vessel were exceedingly remote. On reaching London, they were delighted to learn that accommodation was available on a Danish East Indiaman, the "Kron Princessa Maria," bound from Copenhagen to Calcutta and expected soon off Dover. The cost of passages on the Maria was higher than on the Oxford, and the money which the missionaries had with them was insufficient to cover this extra expense. The Maria's London agent, however, promised to reserve berths for them while they endeavored to raise additional cash. Carey and Thomas dashed off to Northampton for this purpose and on the way stopped at Carey's home in Hackleton. Carey seized the opportunity to attempt once more to persuade his wife to accompany him to India. This time, with the help of Thomas, he was successful, but only after agreeing to Mrs. Carey's stipulation that her sister must go to India as her companion.

Ryland, the Northampton member of the missionary committee, was astonished when Carey and Thomas suddenly appeared at his house and began excitedly to tell him what had happened to them since they bade him farewell shortly after the valedictory service, and to beseech him to provide more money to pay for

five additional passages to India. There was no
time for Ryland to summon a meeting of the
committee, so on his own initiative he gave
them all the mission funds in hand and provided them with letters to friends of his in London, entreating their help for the two missionaries.

Once more Carey and Thomas went to
Hackleton, this time to dispose of Carey's
furniture and such belongings as could not be
taken to India. The party of eight, Thomas,
Carey, Mrs. Carey, Mrs. Carey's sister Catharine Plackett, and the four Carey children
then rushed off to London. Here they were
able to raise more money on the strength of
Ryland's letters, but they still did not have sufficient to pay for eight fares to India, even after
Thomas and Catharine Plackett gallantly offered to travel on the ship as attendants, which
meant a substantial reduction in the cost of
their tickets. The "Maria's" agent, who was
much impressed by the dogged determination
of Carey and Thomas, saved the situation by
generously agreeing to let the missionary party
sail at greatly reduced rates.

All arrangements being satisfactorily con-
cluded, the missionaries and the women and
children were able to embark on the "Kron
Princessa Maria," and set sail for India on
June 13, 1793.

William Carey was thirty-two years old when he went to Bengal as a missionary. He had already amply demonstrated that he possessed certain virtues, such as patience in trying circumstances, tenacity of purpose, the ability to live simply, courage to follow his deepest convictions, faith in the goodness and wisdom and love of God. He had manifested a love for learning, a passion for mastering languages, a devotion to the Word of God. He had proved himself a faithful pastor, an earnest soul-winner, a loyal colleague. But in this act of setting forth as a foreign missionary, Carey was dramatically reminding the Protestant Christian world that our Lord meant the Great Commission to be taken seriously. So successful was Carey in rousing the church to a sense of missionary obligation to the whole world that he is rightly called the father of the modern missionary movement.

Chapter Two

Early Missionary Work in Bengal

T<small>HE</small> <small>VOYAGE</small> of the sailing ship "Kron Princessa Maria" to Calcutta, India, with Carey and his family, Thomas, and four other passengers took from June 13 to November 11, 1793. Captain Christmas, who commanded the vessel, treated the missionary party with much respect and consideration. Daily during the passage to India the missionaries conducted morning and evening worship, and on Sundays held services. Carey spent much time studying the Bengali language under the guidance of Thomas and became so proficient that he was able to help Thomas translate the Book of Genesis into Bengali.

Carey and the others disembarked at Calcutta on November 11, 1793, but found the

cost of living in the city to be so high that they
stayed there only long enough to sell the goods
they had brought with them from England as
a medium of exchange. They then moved
thirty miles north to the Portuguese settlement
of Bandel, accompanied by Dr. Thomas'
former tutor in Bengali, Ram Basu, who acted
as interpreter. The missionaries used Bandel
as a center from which to visit nearby villages
to preach. After a few weeks' residence in
Bandel, Thomas intimated that their funds
were becoming low, so it was decided to return to Calcutta where Carey and Thomas
could seek some form of secular employment.
Thomas was able to resume medical practice
without much difficulty. Carey applied for a
post which had recently fallen vacant, that of
Superintendent of Calcutta's Botanical Gar-
dens, but was unsuccessful in this as in every
other effort to find employment in Calcutta.
By January of 1794, Carey was in desperate
financial straits as the mission's funds, which
according to Thomas' estimate in England
should have been sufficient to maintain the
missionaries for a full year, were totally ex-
pended. A Hindu moneylender came to Carey's
aid by giving him the use, free of charge, of a
small house in Manicktolla, a suburb of Calcutta. Here Carey continued his Bengali studies, his public preaching to Bengalis through

Ram Basu as interpreter, and his personal
work among Bengalis who could understand
English.

In February, 1794, Carey was offered the
use of several acres of land in the Sundarbans,
a tiger- and crocodile-infested area on the Bay
of Bengal, southeast of Calcutta. He accepted
in the hope that he would be able to support
himself and his family through the cultivation
of this land. Upon his arrival at Debhatta on
the Jubuna river in the Sundarbans, Carey and
his family were befriended by an East India
Company assistant in charge of salt manufac-
ture for the area, Mr. Charles Short, who insisted that the well-nigh destitute family be his
guests for as long as they wished. With native
help, Carey began to clear his land at Kalutala,
a mile from Debhatta, and to plant it. He also
commenced the erection of a bamboo house
upon his land, planning to move there upon its
completion.

Carey felt much at home with the Bengali
villagers among whom he lived, and soon won
their confidence because he could be fully
trusted, their admiration because he worked so
hard, and their respect because he spoke to
them so earnestly about the love of God in
Christ. It certainly seemed that the work of the
Baptist Mission was to be firmly established

and built up in the remote jungles of southeast Bengal.

Early in March, 1794, however, Carey received from Mr. George Udny, East India Company Commercial Resident at Malda, through the influence of Dr. Thomas, the offer at a liberal salary of the post of superintendent of an indigo factory in Mudnabati, Dinajpur District, North Bengal, 300 miles from Debhatta. As Carey thought over Mr. Udny's proposition, he became convinced that the hand of God was in it. As superintendent of the Mudnabati Indigo Factory, he would enjoy certain advantages: a large salary plus commission, which would make him completely self-supporting; a commodious, well-built house; a splendid Christian employer who would encourage his missionary ambitions; the East India Company license granting him the right to remain in Bengal; and plenty of leisure, during the indigo off-seasons, to engage in missionary work. Carey therefore decided to abandon his plans for a farm at Kalutala and accept the position in Mudnabati.

It was with much pleasure that Carey wrote to the missionary committee in England to inform them of this latest development and to notify them that since he was about to become self-supporting he would no longer need a salary from them. This action was in keeping with the policy Carey had enunciated in his "Enquiry" to the effect that missionaries should maintain themselves on the mission field.

Carey's departure from Debhatta had to be delayed till May 23, when he received money from Mr. Udny to cover travel expenses to North Bengal. Meanwhile Carey had been reflecting upon his experiences in Debhatta and wrote in his diary:

> O how glorious are the ways of God! My soul longeth and fainteth for God, for the living God, to see His glory and beauty as I have seen them in the sanctuary. When I first left England my hope of the conversion of the heathen was very strong; but, among so many obstacles, it would entirely die away unless upheld by God. Nothing to exercise it, but plenty to obstruct it, for now a year and nineteen days, which is the space since I left my dear charge at Leicester. Since that I have had hurrying up and down; a five months' imprisonment with carnal men on board the ship; five more learning the language; my moonshi (tutor) not understanding English sufficiently to interpret my preaching; my colleague separated from me; long delays and few opportunities for social worship; no woods to retire to, like Brainerd, for fear of tigers (no less than twenty men in the department of Deharta, where I am, have been carried away by them this season from the

salt-works); no earthly thing to depend upon, or earthly comfort, except food and raiment. Well, I have God, and His Word is sure; and though the superstitions of the heathen were a million times worse than they are, if I were deserted by all, and persecuted by all, yet my hope, fixed on that sure Word, will rise superior to all obstructions, and triumph over all trials.[1]

Catharine Plackett, Carey's sister-in-law, did not accompany the Careys to North Bengal but remained in Debhatta to marry Charles Short, the warmhearted East India Company assistant who so wonderfully helped Carey in his time of great need.

The journey to Malda, which was by river, took twenty-three days, and on June 15, 1794, Carey and his family were warmly welcomed to Malda by Mr. Udny. Some days later Carey left for Mudnabati, thirty miles to the north, and here inspected the building of the new indigo factory and the house he was to occupy. Later he returned to Malda, where for several weeks he daily visited indigo factories to learn how to make blue dye by fermenting indigo plants in huge vats and beating the liquid derived therefrom until it precipitated the dye, which then had to be boiled, drained, dried, and packed for shipment to Calcutta and over-

---

[1] Carey's Diary, April 19, 1794.

seas. Also in Malda, whenever Carey happened to be there on Sundays, he conducted services in English for the European residents.

Carey enjoyed his first season in Mudnabati as an indigo planter. He was not without troubles. He suffered a severe attack of malaria which almost cost him his life; his five-year-old son Peter died from malaria; his wife had constant attacks of dysentery, and her mind became unbalanced; he was greatly troubled by the grip idolatry had upon the natives; and he and his family were at times despondent when the mail from England arrived and there was not a single letter for them, an experience which was theirs for the first year and a half in India. Yet in spite of Carey's troubles, his position as Factory Superintendent at Mudnabati gave him innumerable opportunities to meet Bengalis in all walks of life; his business travels throughout the district made him thoroughly acquainted with the land and the people; his large salary made it possible for him to provide generously for the needs of his family and also to meet the expenses of the missionary work in which he engaged; his substantial house permitted him to live in comparative comfort; his large garden allowed him to indulge his hobby of botany and to grow plants which he ordered from overseas; and above all the leisure time at his disposal when the fac-

tory closed for the season afforded him the opportunity of going from village to village to
preach the glorious Gospel and also of working on the translation of the Bible into Bengali.

From the time of his arrival in India, Carey
wrote regularly to the missionary committee in
England and furnished the committee with a
detailed report of every significant event in his
life and work in Bengal. These reports were
widely published in England and created great
interest in the Bengal mission. One communi-
cation from Carey caused the committee grave
concern, namely the letter which informed
them of his appointment as superintendent of
the Mudnabati Indigo Factory at a salary of
approximately £250 per annum, that is, a
salary much larger than any member of the
committee earned. The committee decided to
warn Carey to exercise much caution "lest he
should allow the spirit of the missionary to be
swallowed up in the pursuits of the merchant."
Carey resented this admonition for several
good reasons: the committee knew that he had
gone to India as a missionary on the distinct
understanding that he would become self-supporting as soon as possible; the committee had
been lax in sending him funds and he and his
family would have been in a desperate plight
had he depended solely upon their help; and
the committee failed to appreciate that he was

devoting almost one-third of his salary for
missionary work. From his own pocket Carey
met the following expenses: the cost of the
upkeep of an excellent village school for promising Bengali children, and the teacher's salary;
the salaries of the men who tutored him in
Bengali and Sanskrit and helped in translation
work; payment to men who made copies by
hand of certain portions of Scripture for free
distribution; the cost of the large supply of
paper needed in translation work; and the total
expenses of all the touring in the villages to
preach the Gospel.

Carey had good reasons to be encouraged
by the progress he was making in translating
the Bible into Bengali, for by the summer of
1796, when less than three years in the country, he had almost completed the translation of
the New Testament as well as a substantial part
of the Pentateuch. Carey was, however, deeply
disappointed that he had not made similar
headway in winning converts. He had high
hopes that his tutor, Ram Basu, would become
a Christian, for Basu was undoubtedly better
acquainted with the facts of the Gospel than
any other Bengali. Basu was well acquainted
with the Word of God, having helped Carey
translate it, he had helped to preach the Gospel
time and time again by acting as interpreter
for both Thomas and Carey, and he had even

written a Bengali hymn, the theme of which was

> O who, save Jesus, can deliver us
> From the eternal darkness of sin?

Yet he was never willing to make public profession of faith in Christ. The only convert during Carey's ministry in North Bengal was not a Bengali but a Roman Catholic of Portuguese descent, Ignatius Fernandez from Macao, who had settled in India and become a wealthy cloth and candle merchant in the town of Dinajpur. He became a loyal Baptist and an enthusiastic supporter of the Baptist Mission. It was he who built the first Baptist Chapel in North Bengal.

Carey's distress at the complete failure to make any converts from Hinduism or Islam caused him to renew his pleas to the missionary committee to send reinforcements, for he was convinced that a group of missionaries working in close association would be able to accomplish what he had failed to do single-handed. Carey's plans called for the establishing in North Bengal of a missionary community of seven or eight families who would live, eat, work, and worship together. All earnings would be turned into a common pool from which the expenses of the group would be met. Each missionary and his family would live in a mud house with a thatched roof, the houses being built in close proximity to facilitate corporate life. Concerning this scheme of Carey's, Marshman makes the observation:

> The primitive simplicity and self-denial of this plan exhibited the zeal and devotion to the cause which always animated him, but it was no proof of the soundness of his judgment. Even if his straw huts and mud floors had not sent half the community to the grave during the first rainy season, the inconceivable distress to which European families must have been subjected in such a colony, in such a climate, would have broken it up within a twelve-month.[2]

Despite Carey's appeals, the home committee sent only one additional missionary during the first six years of the mission in Bengal, John Fountain, a lay missionary, who was an excellent companion for Carey in Mudnabati, but displayed little competence as a missionary. Early in 1799, however, Carey received word from England that more missionaries would shortly be joining him, and it appeared the home committee expected him to put his scheme for a mission settlement into effect. This news came when he was facing an unusually serious situation, for he had been in-

---

[2] Marshman, *The Life and Labours of Carey, Marshman and Ward*, p. 33.

formed by his employer, Mr. Udny, that the
Mudnabati factory was to be shut down perma-
nently and his services as manager were to be
terminated. For three seasons floods and
drought had caused havoc in the indigo fields
in the Malda area and Mr. Udny had, in consequence, suffered severe losses. Carey's scheme
for a self-supporting mission community of
seven or eight families in North Bengal had
been devised when he was receiving, as an
indigo planter, a salary large enough to be a
significant contribution to the common fund
needed to maintain the missionary group, so
the loss of his excellent position at Mudnabati
was a severe blow to Carey's plans. Carey
made a bold decision, namely to buy an indigo
factory at Khidurpur, twelve miles north of
Mudnabati, and establish the mission settlement there. The profits from the Khidurpur
Factory would, it was hoped, maintain the
Mission. Carey invested every penny of his savings in the purchase of this factory, and also
borrowed heavily from Mr. Udny.

Meanwhile, the missionaries for whom
Carey was making these preparations were on
their way to India aboard the S. S. "Criterion,"
an American ship commanded by Captain
Wickes, a Presbyterian elder from Philadel-
phia. The missionary party included three families, the Grants, the Brunsdons, and the

Marshmans; one bachelor, William Ward; and
Fountain's fiancée, Miss Tidd. Before leaving
London, the missionaries had been advised by
one of the East India Company directors,
godly Charles Grant, not to disembark in Cal-
cutta, where their presence without East India
Company licenses would almost certainly result in their deportation, but to go immediately
to Serampore, a small Danish settlement on the
Hoogly River, sixteen miles from Calcutta.
Grant reasoned that in Serampore the missionaries would be under the jurisdiction of the
Danish authorities and that no action, therefore, could be taken against them by the East
India Company so long as they remained in
Serampore. The missionaries followed Grant's
advice and landed in Serampore on October
13, 1799. They received a cordial welcome
from the Danish officials and a firm assurance
of protection from the Danish governor, Colonel Bie. When Carey learned of their arrival he
sent Fountain to welcome them and to acquaint
them with his plans for them in North Bengal.
He then made every effort to persuade the East
India Company to license the four missionaries as indigo planters who would work with
him at the factory in North Bengal, but was
unsuccessful. The missionaries at Serampore,
after conferring with Fountain, decided that
Ward should obtain a Danish passport and, in

company with Fountain, travel to Mudnabati
to talk over the situation with Carey. Fountain
and Ward arrived in Mudnabati on December 1 and had lengthy discussions with Carey
concerning the location of the mission. There
were good reasons why the mission should remain in North Bengal. It owned an indigo factory which, if successfully operated, would
supply all the funds needed to maintain the missionaries and their families; it had a well-estab-
lished and popular school for Bengali boys,
who were being taught the facts of Christianity;
it was an area where Carey had won the confidence and respect of Hindus and Muslims;
and it was a region where for six years Carey
had preached the Gospel in village after village, and there was good reason to expect a
harvest of souls here. There were, however, at
this particular time, certain disadvantages in
remaining in North Bengal: Carey's new colleagues were unable to settle in North Bengal
since the East India Company had refused
them permission; Carey had no guarantee that
his own license to remain in North Bengal
would be renewed; and it was obvious to Carey
that the Khidurpur indigo factory might prove
a liability to the mission if there were poor
indigo seasons. There were certainly excellent
reasons for the mission to move to Serampore:
there was Colonel Bie's warm invitation to the

Baptists freely to engage in missionary work in Serampore; in Serampore town there was plenty of property which the mission could rent or purchase; Serampore was an excellent place for the printing of the Scriptures since supplies of type, paper, and ink were easily obtainable; at Serampore the mission would be near Calcutta, the political, cultural, and educational center of Bengal and the rest of India; and in Serampore the missionaries would be beyond the control of the British authorities who were hostile to missionary work.

Carey was undoubtedly perplexed whether to stay in North Bengal or go to Serampore, but on the day following his discussions with Fountain and Ward he informed his two colleagues that he definitely felt it to be God's will that the mission be established in Serampore. On January 1, 1800, Carey and his family, along with Fountain and Ward, set out for Serampore, which they reached on January 10. Dr. Thomas, whose relationship to the mission had become tenuous, did not accompany them.

Carey commenced this new phase of missionary life and work in Serampore with a wonderful background of knowledge and experience. He had mastered three of India's languages, Bengali, Sanskrit, and Hindustani. He had translated the whole Bible, except for a few chapters, into Bengali, and had it ready for the printer. He had become an expert preacher in Bengali. Through his experience as superintendent of the Mudnabati indigo factory he was a skilled administrator. He possessed extensive knowledge of the habits and customs of Bengalis. He was considered an authority on the flora of North Bengal. He was well acquainted, through the schools he managed, with the problems of education in Bengal. He had acquired a fund of knowledge about tropical diseases and their treatment. And he had learned in the midst of many trials and testings that "the Lord is good; his mercy is everlasting." [3]

---

[3] Psalm 100:5.

Chapter Three

Serampore, 1800-1813

ON JANUARY 10, 1800, Carey arrived at Serampore and met the others who
had traveled to British India with Ward,
namely the Brunsdons, the Marshmans, and
Mrs. Grant. Mr. Grant had died from an attack of fever soon after his arrival in India.
Carey's first task in Serampore was to call
upon the governor, Col. Bie, and express warm
appreciation for the sanctuary he had given the
Baptist Mission. His second task was to secure
housing for himself and his fellow missionaries.
This was no easy task, for the group now con-
sisted of ten adults and nine children. Carey
quickly realized that while it might have been
feasible for missionaries and their families sta-
tioned in the remote jungles of North Bengal
to reside in mud huts, this would not be prac-
ticable in the Serampore area where there were
many Europeans living in well-built brick

houses. He took the bold step of purchasing a commodious house and estate costing £800. The house had a spacious hall, which was made into a chapel. Other rooms in the house were allocated to the various missionary families. A separate storehouse became the site of the mission printing press. Carey was given charge of the estate grounds, and these he beautified with trees, flowers and shrubs. Within six months he had planted 427 species of plants. In his Serampore garden Carey eventually had the rarest and best collection of plants in the East.

Rules for the missionary community were prepared by Carey and adopted by his colleagues. It was agreed that each missionary would take his turn in acting as superintendent of the mission for a month; the missionaries and their families would dine together at a common table; the missionary community would be supported by the earnings of its members, all income being credited to a common treasury, with each family receiving a small allowance for personal expenses; and on Saturday all would gather at a special session to settle, in the spirit of Christian love, any differences which might have arisen during the week. In uniting secular occupation with missionary work Carey was not inaugurating a new policy, for missionaries connected with the S.P.C.K., namely Schwarz, Gericke, and Kiernander, had never depended upon the missionary society at home for their entire financial support, but they supplemented the society's allowance by their own earnings in India. The Serampore missionaries did, however, adopt a new principle by divesting themselves of the right of property in their own earnings and devoting this income exclusively to missionary work through a common fund.

Carey's colleagues, the Marshmans and William Ward, loyally endorsed his policy of making the mission self-supporting. In May, 1800, the Marshmans opened boarding schools at Serampore to help mission funds. By the end of two years profits from these schools had risen to 1,000 rupees per month. Ward had set up the printing press with the primary object of printing the Bible and Gospel tracts, but he also undertook printing for government and the general public, and income from work of this nature steadily grew. The finances of the mission were further greatly strengthened when in May of 1801 Carey became teacher of Bengali in the government College of Fort William, Calcutta, at a monthly salary of 500 rupees. Some years later Carey was promoted to a professorship in this college, and his salary was increased to 1,000 rupees per month. All of this money was put into the common fund.

In spite of the assured financial position en-

joyed by the Serampore mission, Carey and his
colleagues practiced the strictest economy in
household and personal expenses. They and
their families and the boarders from the Marshmans' schools all dined together. Ward noted:

> We live moderately and drink only rum and
> water. We have always a little cheap fruit:
> goats' flesh—the same as mutton—broth,
> fowls, with a little beef sometimes, and curry,
> but we have good wheaten bread.[1]

Though the Baptist Mission at Serampore
had attained financial independence, Carey
encouraged the home committee of the B.M.S.
to send grants-in-aid. Of the total expenses of
the mission at Serampore for the first five years,
namely £13,000, £5,741 came from the society in England. This policy gave the missionaries freedom of action, and they were able,
without reference to the society at home, to enlarge the sphere of their work, purchase buildings, erect churches, and appoint missionaries
raised up in India. The practice of devoting all
they earned to missionary work won for Carey
and his colleagues the admiration of Christian
people in India, England, and America, and
stimulated the flow of missionary giving. The
self-sacrificial example set by the Serampore

---

[1] Marshman, *The Life and Times of Carey, Marshman and Ward*. Vol. I, p. 152.

missionaries was followed by many of their
converts. For example, a convert in North
Bengal, Fernandez, was ordained as a missionary, but he also continued to supervise the factories he owned, devoting the profits to missionary work.

From a financial aspect the communal
system of living adopted by the Baptist missionaries at Carey's suggestion was successful,
but in the realm of personal relationships the
scheme did not have similar success. By July,
1801, of the six missionaries who had adopted
the rules for communal living, there were only
three survivors, Carey, Marshman, and Ward.
These three seemed well adapted to each other
and lived in close harmony. The situation
changed with the arrival in Serampore of several new missionaries, one in 1803 and four in
1805. Dissatisfaction arose among the new missionaries because, on the ground of their inex-
perience, they were not permitted an equal
share in the management of the mission. Feel-
ings were aroused, and there was much correspondence on the subject between Serampore
and the home committee. The committee in
England had, from the first time they learned
of it, disagreed with Carey's policy that every
missionary was entitled to an equal share in
the management of the mission. In 1807 the
missionaries decided that they and their fami-

lies should live communally only by their own
consent, and that the distinct families should
constitute a general mission with a committee
and a secretary to transact business. This new
arrangement did not succeed, however, as the
junior missionaries still objected to the control
of affairs exercised by their senior colleagues.
The dispute was ended, at least openly, when
the home committee notified all concerned that
the management of the Baptist Mission in
Bengal was to be vested in Carey, Marshman,
and Ward for their lifetime. By insisting, in
1805, that experience be the determining
factor in deciding who should manage the mission, Carey revealed a change in opinion. In
1800 he had admitted Marshman, Ward, and
the others to equal partnership in the affairs of
the mission even though they had newly arrived in the country and were totally inexperi-
enced in missionary matters. Carey's later view-
point failed sufficiently to appreciate that it was
somewhat unreasonable to expect missionaries
and their families to conform to a system of
communal living, yet deny them the privilege
of an equal share in the management of community life and work. One of the junior missionaries, Johns, in a series of letters entitled
"The Spirit of the Serampore System" points
out in Letter 2 that the senior missionaries who
arranged for him to be appointed government

surgeon in Serampore received all his salary
and private fees into the common fund, expected him to take his meals at the common
table, but did not admit him to equal partnership in the system.

Other problems which faced Carey in the
early years at Serampore arose out of the rela-
tion of missionaries to government. He and his
colleagues had settled in Serampore in order to
carry on missionary work under the protection
of the Danish government, which controlled
Serampore. Danish officials in Serampore
treated the Baptist missionaries with the greatest respect and courtesy and extended to them
all the privileges of Danish citizenship, including Danish passports which permitted the missionaries to travel in areas controlled by the
East India Company. Carey was most grateful
for these favors, and at a special day of thanks-
giving on April 24, 1800, he and the others decided to send a letter of gratitude to the king
of Denmark.

On May 8, 1801, an event took place which
might have proved disastrous to the Baptist
Mission. War had broken out between Denmark and Britain, so the English Governor-
General in Calcutta took possession of Serampore. The missionaries there were no longer
under the protection of the Danish government, and the East India Company officials

could have deported them. Hough portrays
what actually happened:

> The missionaries were desired to appear at
> the Government House, where the English
> Commissioner behaved to them with great
> civility, apologised for the trouble he had
> given them, and assured them that they were
> at perfect liberty to follow their calling as
> usual.[2]

It was obviously not the policy of the government constantly to interfere with missionary
work on the mere pretext of disliking it. During the years 1800-1813 there were only three
occasions when the East India Company officially placed restrictions upon Carey and his
colleagues: in 1806 when the Vellore Mutiny,
in which 113 officers and men of the English
garrison were massacred by Sepoys, was considered an indirect result of missionary efforts
to convert Hindus; in 1807 when the Serampore missionaries inadvertently published a
tract which used offensive language concerning the prophet Muhammad and which the
government therefore considered inflammatory
and dangerous; and in 1812 when the government felt forced to take action against missionaries because certain important Indian princes

---

[2] Hough, *History of Christianity in India*. Vol. IV,
p. 115.

such as the Dowlat Scindia had registered formal protests against missionary work.

Carey had great cause for rejoicing in 1813 when the new charter granted by the British Parliament to the East India Company included an important resolution concerning Christianity in India. One part of the resolution, the adoption of which ensured that missionaries would be permitted to reside in India and to engage in missionary work without interference from the government, reads as follows:

> XIII RESOLVED. That it is the opinion of this Committee that it is the duty of this country to promote the interest and happiness of the native inhabitants of the British dominions in India, and that such measures ought to be adopted as may tend to the introduction among them of useful knowledge and of religious and moral improvement. That in the furtherance of the above objects sufficient facilities shall be afforded by law to persons desirous of going to, and remaining in, India for the purpose of accomplishing these benevolent designs.[3]

There had been much bitter opposition by many members of Parliament to this resolution on Christianity, but the House could not ignore British public sentiment, which strongly favored it. When the Charter Act of 1813 was

---

[3] Missionary Register, 1813, p. 236.

being debated in Parliament, one of the members, Wilberforce, spoke in glowing terms of Carey's excellent missionary work. There can be little doubt that the high esteem and affection in which Carey and his colleagues were held by British people in India and in Britain greatly helped to bring about the passing of an act which officially permitted missionary work in India.

None of the problems which faced Carey in his early years at Serampore seriously interfered with what he considered the first essential condition of the evangelization of India, namely the translation of the Bible into India's vernacular languages, a task he had made his chief interest. He wrote on Dec. 22, 1796:

> The translation of the Scriptures I look upon to be one of the greatest desiderata in the world, and it has accordingly occupied a considerable part of my time and attention.[4]

As has already been noted, the attention of Carey was directed first to the translation of the Bible into Bengali, and he completed his translation of the New Testament in 1797. By 1800 he had translated the Old Testament except for two books. On February 7, 1801, Ward was able to announce with great joy that he had finished printing the first copy of the Bengali

---

[4] Periodical Accounts, Vol. I, p. 345.

New Testament. In 1803 a new edition of the Bengali New Testament was printed. It was almost a new translation rather than an improvement of the first edition. Carey's position as teacher of Bengali at the College of Fort William brought him into contact with some of the most eminent of India's scholars and, with their help, he produced a more accurate and idiomatic translation. Carey also took advantage of the presence of Indian scholars at Fort William to learn other Indian languages, and between 1803 and 1806 he began translating the New Testament into Hindi, Oriya, Sanskrit, and Marathi. In 1809 Carey reported remarkable progress in translation: the whole Bible had now been printed in Bengali; the Bengali New Testament was in its third and improved edition; the New Testament had been printed in Oriya and Sanskrit; the translation of the New Testament into Marathi and Gujarati had been completed, but printing held up for lack of funds; and a rough translation of the New Testament in Telugu and Punjabi had been done.

Carey's translation program suffered a serious blow on March 11, 1812, when a fire in the printing office at Serampore destroyed valuable manuscripts, books, and type. The damage was estimated at £10,000 (then approximately close to $50,000), but when news reached England of the disaster the entire sum was raised in fifty days.

The extent of Carey's prodigious labours in the translation of the Bible during his first twenty years as a missionary may be summed up as follows: the Bible translated and printed in Bengali; the New Testament translated and printed in Bengali, Sanskrit, Oriya, Marathi and Hindi; the New Testament translated but not printed in Telugu, Kanarese, Gujarati and Punjabi; and work begun on a translation into Kashmiri. Concerning these achievements Sherring writes:

> In no country in the world, and in no period of the history of Christianity was there ever displayed such an amount of energy in the translation of the sacred Scriptures from their originals into other tongues, as was exhibited by a handful of earnest men in Calcutta and Serampore in the first ten years of the present century (the 19th c.) . . . It cannot be supposed that these first attempts are to be compared with the versions which have been subsequently made in these languages. But this must not diminish the intense admiration we ought to feel towards men of such boldness of design and such astounding energy of execution.[5]

Carey's enthusiasm for preaching the Word

[5] Sherring, *Protestant Missions in India*, pp. 85, 86.

of God matched his enthusiasm for translating it. In North Bengal he had seized every opportunity to make tours through the villages to preach the Gospel. Cox notes: "Carey proceeded in perpetual rotation through two hundred villages to proclaim the Gospel." [6]

In 1799 Carey wrote: "I preach every day to the natives." [7]

At Serampore open-air evangelism was begun in 1800, and morning and evening Carey and Fountain preached in the streets of the town. Frequently at these meetings there would be discussions when educated Bengalis expressed disagreement with the message proclaimed by the missionaries that only in Christ is there salvation. The theme of their preaching was formally stated by Carey and his colleagues in 1805 when they drew up a form of agreement (Form of Agreement respecting the Great Principles upon which the Brethren of the Mission at Serampore think it their duty to act in the work of instructing the Heathen, agreed upon at a Meeting of the Brethren at Serampore on Monday, October 7, 1805).

In preaching to the heathen, we must keep to the example of Paul, and make the great sub-

---

[6] Cox, *History of the Baptist Missionary Society*. Vol. I, p. 34.

[7] Marshman, *The Life and Times of Carey, Marshman and Ward*. Vol. I, p. 89.

ject of our preaching, Christ the Crucified.
. . . The doctrine of Christ's expiatory death
and all-sufficient merits has been, and must
ever remain, the grand means of conversion.[8]

The Serampore missionaries preached with
a sense of urgency because of their conviction
that people without Christ are eternally lost.
Their views are recorded in the Form of Agreement:

> In order to be prepared for our great and
> solemn work it is absolutely necessary that
> we set an infinite value upon immortal souls;
> that we often endeavour to affect our minds
> with the dreadful loss sustained by an uncon-
> verted soul launched into eternity. It becomes
> us to fix in our minds the awful doctrine of
> eternal punishment, and to realise frequently
> the inconceivably awful condition of this vast
> country, lying in the arms of the wicked one.
> If we have not this awful sense of the value
> of souls, it is impossible that we can feel
> aright in any other part of our work, and in
> this case it had been better for us to have
> been in any other situation rather than in
> that of a missionary.[9]

Carey was firmly convinced of the value of
Gospel tracts in the work of evangelism. The

---

[8] Serampore Form of Agreement, 1805.
[9] *Ibid.*

first Bengali tract distributed by the Baptist
Mission was written, at Carey's request, by
Ram Basu, a talented Bengali who was deeply
interested in Christianity but who never himself became a Christian. In this tract, "The
Gospel Messenger," Basu introduced the
Gospel to his countrymen. Thereafter the missionaries and their converts wrote tracts and
distributed them on every possible occasion.
The interest aroused by these tracts was great,
and a steady stream of Bengalis visited Serampore for further information about Christianity. Tracts, however, were not always gladly
received; at times they were torn to pieces after
being distributed, either before the missionary's eyes or after his departure.

The use of schools as a means of evangelism
was a policy initiated by Carey early in his missionary career, and when he left North Bengal
for Serampore in 1799 Carey was able to report
that fifty boys had been taught reading and
writing and knew something of Christian truth.
In Serampore and the surrounding district, free
schools were opened by the missionaries as
means of "diffusing the knowledge of the
Gospel." At the end of ten years there were
sixteen schools with a total attendance of one
thousand.

These methods of evangelism, preaching,
teaching, and the distribution of Bibles and

tracts began to bear fruit. The first Bengali
won from Hinduism to Christ by the Baptist
missionaries was a carpenter, Krishna Chandra
Pal. Dr. Thomas had treated Pal for a dislo-
cated shoulder and at the same time had
preached Christ to him. After a month's instruction in Christian doctrine, Krishna Pal
announced his intention to renounce Hinduism and become a Christian. This decision
caused a sensation among the Hindus of Serampore, and a large mob of agitators tried to
force Krishna Pal to change his mind, but he
was adamant. He was baptized by Carey in
the River Hoogly on December 28, 1800 before a large crowd of Hindus and Muslims. The
baptism of the first Bengali women upon profession of faith in Christ took place some
months later. The women were Krishna Pal's
wife and his sister-in-law. These conversions
were followed by others, including that of the
first Brahmin to become a Christian, Krishna
Prasad; and by the end of 1803 forty baptisms
had taken place.

The Serampore missionaries sought to im-
press upon their converts the need for them to
evangelize their own countrymen. At a meeting of converts held in Serampore on August
8, 1806, Carey and his colleagues drew the attention of Bengali Christians to the following
points:

1. That the intention of their Saviour in calling them out of darkness into marvellous light, was that they should labour to the uttermost in advancing His cause among their countrymen.
2. That it was therefore their indispensable duty, both collectively and individually, to strive by every means to bring their countrymen to the knowledge of the Saviour; that if we, who were strangers, thought it our duty to come from a country so distant for this purpose, much more was it incumbent on them to labour for the same end.[10]

Most converts seemed eager to engage in evangelism. Because of secular occupation many of them were unable to give time for this on weekdays. On Sundays, however, nearly every Bengali Christian connected with the Baptist Church preached the Gospel in some village or another near Serampore. The Serampore missionaries acknowledged the numerical growth of the Serampore church to be due to the efforts of Bengali converts rather than to their own efforts.

When it became possible for the Baptist missionaries to do evangelistic work in British India and to go on evangelistic tours, they made it a practice to take along Bengali Chris-

---

[10] Smith, *Life of William Carey*, p. 167.

tians who had demonstrated special skill in preaching. From this evangelistic activity were developed preaching centers and mission stations at the following places: Calcutta, 1801; Jessore, 1805; Malda, 1806 and Agra, 1811. Some of the Serampore junior missionaries went even farther afield, to Burma in 1807 and to Ceylon in 1812.

The creation of an Indian Christian community in Serampore through the evangelistic efforts of the missionaries there naturally led to the formulation of policy with respect to converts. Carey was largely responsible for the measures which were adopted. Hindu candidates for baptism were required to renounce caste. Caste has been defined by Freytag as:

> The unit of life in which the Indian exists, and which so lays its stamp on his whole existence, that he cannot really live without it. A man is born into a certain caste and there are said to be between 2000 and 3000 of them. . . . Caste not only determines a man's rank, and keeps him strictly apart from other castes by strict endogamy, forbidding him to eat with members of another caste, but in the majority of cases it also determines his profession. . . . Inheritance and marriage rites, the dress and the habits of daily life, prohibitions in eating, the honour paid to the deceased, and religious observances, everything is mapped out for the

Hindu at his birth, inevitably and irrevocably.[11]

The first converts in Serampore signified the renunciation of caste by eating food with the missionaries. Brahmin converts renounced caste by trampling on the *poita,* or sacred thread, the emblem of Brahminhood. In requiring such renunciation before acceptance into the church, Carey adopted a policy contrary to that of German and Danish missionaries in South India who permitted caste distinctions in the churches they established. Carey made every effort to ensure that the distinctions of caste did not enter into the life of the Baptist Church in India. At the celebration of the Lord's Supper, converts formerly of high caste received the bread and wine after converts of low caste. Marriage between converts formerly of different castes was encouraged. Converts were asked to assist in tasks which were previously forbidden them by caste rules, as for example, when a baptized Brahmin (the highest caste) was requested to help carry the body of a baptized Sudra (the lowest caste) to the cemetery.

Though Carey and his colleagues took this definite stand against caste, they made it clear

---

[11] Freytag, *Spiritual Revolution in the East,* p. 134.

that they had no desire unnecessarily to interfere with the habits and customs of converts.

> We think the great object which Divine Providence has in view in causing the Gospel to be promulgated in the world is not the change of names, the dress, the food, and the innocent usages of mankind, but to produce a moral and divine change in the hearts and conduct of men.[12]

It was with this in mind that the Serampore missionaries decided not to give Christian names to converts at baptism.

> Mr. Carey opposed the practice (of giving names at baptism); not only because he could perceive no necessary connection between the rite of baptism and a change of name, but also because it did not appear to have been usual in the apostolic age to repudiate such names of heathen origin as Sylvanus, Olympias, Hermes, Nereus and Fortunatus.[13]

The question of converts with several wives had to be dealt with by Carey. He decided that a convert with more than one wife should not be compelled to put away any of them but that so long as he remained in a polygamous state he was disqualified from any office in the church.

---

[12] Marshman, *The Life and Times of Carey, Marshman and Ward.* Vol. I, p. 176.
[13] *Ibid.* Vol. I, p. 151.

Another question of policy concerned converts whose wives refused to join them. In 1804 there were two such converts in this position. One of them, a young Brahmin, repeatedly attempted to persuade his wife that though he had become a Christian he still considered himself her husband, but she flatly refused to live with him. He asked the missionaries for advice.

> Carey and his colleagues after maturely weighing the circumstances of the case determined in accordance with the decision of St. Paul:—"But if the unbelieving depart, let him depart. A brother or a sister is not under bondage in such a case"—that the convert was no longer debarred from contracting a second marriage.[14]

Many converts found it exceedingly difficult, after baptism, to secure employment since they were no longer members of their caste. So enthusiastic had Carey and his fellow missionaries been about their first converts that at baptism they presented to each a new cloth or a dress, and a sum of money. They bought a house for one convert. As converts increased, the missionaries realized they had established a precedent which was proving financially embarrassing, so the practice of giving gifts at baptism was discontinued. In addition, Carey

---

[14] *Ibid.* Vol. I, p. 285.

urged that financial help should not be given converts unless absolutely necessary, for it was his experience that when converts were thrown upon their own resources they managed in one way or another to earn a livelihood.

On April 24, 1800, the Baptist missionaries formed a church at Serampore, and Bengali converts after baptism enjoyed all the privileges of membership in this church. Services were conducted in Bengali, and hymns were sung from a Bengali hymnbook compiled in 1802, either to English or Indian tunes.

The Serampore missionaries, though happy to have their converts as members with them of the parent Baptist Church in Bengal, began to look forward to the day when Indian Christians would be formed into their own churches throughout the land. Carey and his colleagues felt that three principles should govern such churches: First, such churches must be self-governed.

> We think it our duty, as soon as possible, to advise the native brethren who may be formed into separate Churches to choose their pastors and deacons from amongst their own countrymen, that the Word may be statedly preached, and the ordinances of Christ administered, in each Church by the native minister.[15]

---

[15] Serampore Form of Agreement.

Second, such churches should be self-supporting.

> The different native Churches will also nat-
> urally learn to care and provide for their
> ministers, for their Church expenses, the
> raising of places of worship, etc.[16]

Third, such churches should be self-propa-
gating.

> If . . . a number of native Churches be
> thus established, from them the Word of God
> may sound out even to the extremities of
> India; and numbers of preachers being raised
> up and sent forth, may form a body of na-
> tive missionaries.[17]

Carey tried to make the church, not the
mission, the vital factor in the life and work of
converts.

Carey manifested loving concern for the
spiritual needs of those among whom he lived
and worked; he also displayed a deep and
abiding interest in the physical, intellectual
and moral welfare of the people of India. Soon
after his arrival in North Bengal he had begun
to find out how he could improve agriculture
there and had sent home for seeds of flowers,
vegetables, and trees, stating that he hoped to

---

[16] *Ibid.*
[17] *Ibid.*

use them in introducing new varieties to Bengal. In Serampore Carey continued botanical experiments and made the results of his research known to botanists in India and other parts of the world.

When Carey began missionary work in India, Bengali had no printed and hardly any written literature. This presented a problem to Carey when he commenced his lectures as teacher of Bengali in the College of Fort William, for not a single prose work in Bengali was available. Under Carey's direction a talented Bengali, Ram Basu, compiled a history of Pratapaditya, the last king of Sagar Island. This was published in 1801 and may be regarded as the first prose work printed in Bengali. At this time Carey compiled a Bengali grammar for the use of his students.

Carey did not, however, confine his literary interest to Bengali works. With the help of Marshman he translated the Ramayana, India's most renowned epic, from Sanskrit into English. In 1806 Carey published his Sanskrit grammar.

While Carey in every possible way revealed a genuine interest in the life and the languages of the people of India, and while he made it a point to cultivate the friendliest of relationships with the Hindus and Muslims among whom he worked, he felt it his duty publicly to condemn certain Hindu practices, namely infanticide and suttee. Infanticide was prevalent at the time Carey came to Serampore. It was the custom for Hindu couples who were childless after having been married for several years to make a vow that if they had children they would sacrifice the firstborn to some deity. The sacrifice usually took place at an annual festival held at the spot where the Ganges river joins the sea. Here young children were forced by parents into the water until the sea carried them away. Carey drew up a report on infanticide and urged the government to prohibit the practice. A member of the Governor's Council read Carey's report to the council which, after much deliberation, issued orders in 1802 that the practice of infanticide was forbidden.

Suttee, the practice by which a Hindu widow was burned alive on her husband's funeral pyre, was also practiced in Bengal at this time. An investigation conducted by Carey in 1803 to find out how many widows in an area within thirty miles of Calcutta had been burned alive that year showed the number to be 438. A similar investigation conducted the following year revealed that three hundred widows had been burned alive. Carey presented to the Governor-General, Lord Wellesley, a full report on the subject of suttee and urged the government to forbid the practice. Twenty-five years passed before the government took action in this matter.

By 1813, when the British Parliament approved the East India Company Charter Bill which contained the clauses on Christianity in India, guaranteeing to Christian missionaries freedom to work in India, Carey had been twelve years in Serampore. During this period, he had sustained great personal sorrow: the two colleagues who laboured with him in North Bengal had died, Fountain in 1800 and Dr. Thomas in 1801, and his wife had died in 1807 after much suffering. He had also experienced much personal joy: three of his sons had been ordained and had become missionaries; and in 1808 he had married Miss Charlotte Rumohr, who proved a wonderful wife. He had been honored by two distinguished institutions: the Asiatic Society, which admitted him to membership in 1806, and Brown University, which conferred upon him the honorary degree of Doctor of Divinity in 1807. During these first twelve years in Serampore Carey had distinguished himself as a great missionary statesman, an erudite Oriental scholar, a gifted translator, a learned professor, a skilled botanist, a true friend of Bengal and India and, above all, as one willing to sacrifice all for the sake of his Lord and Saviour, Jesus Christ.

Chapter Four

Serampore, 1814-1834

WITH THE PASSING of the East India
Company Charter Act of 1813, Carey and his
colleagues looked forward to a period which
they hoped would surpass all that they had
hitherto accomplished for Christ and His
Church in India. They were now able freely
to engage in the task of evangelism throughout
British India. We have already noted the opening of mission stations in Agra, Dinajpur, Jessore, and in Burma and Ceylon before 1814.
After 1814, stations were established at Dacca,
Monghyr and Patna in 1816; Delhi in 1818;
Howrah in 1821; Cuttack in 1822; Berhampur
and Puri in 1825; and Barisal in 1828. These
mission stations were staffed by European missionaries recruited from overseas or in India
itself, Anglo-Indians, and Indian nationals.
Carey could now count on receiving missionary
reinforcements from England without interfer-

ence from the East India Company, and he was justifiably pleased that the first of the Baptist missionaries to arrive under the new arrangement was his nephew Eustace.

Carey no longer engaged in open-air preaching. His duties as professor at the College of Fort William and his great translation projects left him little time for itinerant evangelism. He continued, however, to be a keen personal evangelist and gladly welcomed the opportunity of preaching Christ to the many inquirers who came to his office or home.

It was in the period under consideration that the work of Carey in translating the Bible into Bengali and other languages of India reached its climax. In 1832 the Serampore Mission announced that during the years 1801-1832 the Serampore Press had printed 212,000 volumes in forty languages. Carey was responsible for translating the Bible or portions thereof into the following languages or dialects: Bengali, Sanskrit, Oriya, Hindi, Marathi, Punjabi, Bolochi, Mewari, Telugu, Konkani, Pashto, Assamese, Lahnda, Gujerati, Bikaneri, Awadhi, Kashmiri, Nepali, Bagheli, Marawari, Harauti, Kanouji, Kanarese, Jaipuri, Kumaoni, Sindhi, Dogri, Bhatneri, Magahi, Malvi, Braj Brasha, Garwhali, Manipuri, Palpa, and Khasi.

Carey's policy in extending the scope of his

translation endeavors to include so many languages and dialects has been the subject of
varying degrees of criticism. J. S. M. Hooper,
Secretary in India for the British and Foreign
Bible Society, declared about the above policy:

> There can be no doubt that this policy in-
> volved an enormous waste of energy. . . .
> Neither their own qualifications, great though
> they were, nor the resources of Indian schol-
> arship then available, nor indeed the state
> of philological knowledge were sufficient to
> justify Carey and his colleagues in attempt-
> ing the translation of the Scriptures into so
> many different languages.[1]

Julius Richter also criticizes Carey's translation policy:

> It must be frankly admitted that not one of
> these Serampore versions is in use today.
> Soon after their publication, even, some were
> found to be inaccurate in language and im-
> perfect in idiom, and some indeed were so
> faulty that they had to be replaced by com-
> pletely new versions. Even the best of them,
> such as Carey's Bengali and Sanskrit Bibles
> have been so thoroughly revised by gifted
> linguists of later times, that they may almost
> be termed new versions.[2]

---

[1] Hooper, *The Bible in India,* p. 17.
[2] Richter, *History of Missions in India,* p. 139.

While it is a fact that the Serampore versions
have been superseded by others more accurate
and idiomatic, it is surely not logical to infer
from this that Carey followed a wrong policy
or that he wasted his energy. Any evaluation
of Carey's translation policy must keep in mind
the following considerations: (1) Carey was
himself a brilliant translator, but in addition,
he had, at the College of Fort William, the
help of gifted nationals from all parts of India.
(2) It must not be imagined that because much
of Carey's work has been superseded, his translations were of poor quality. Referring to
Carey's last edition of the Bengali Bible, the
late Dr. Howells of Serampore College stated:

> In the judgment of many this final version of
> Carey's has not been surpassed in simplicity
> of style and correctness of idiom.[3]

(3) Too little attention has been paid to the
stimulus given to Indian languages by Carey's
translations. The interest aroused among Indians by reason of the introduction of printed
works in their own languages was tremendous,
and it was this interest which led to the subsequent development of philological studies. In
view of facts brought to light in the course of
such studies, it is not surprising that Carey's
translations were superseded. It is surely, how-

---

[3] Quoted in S. Pearce Carey's *William Carey*, p. 378.

ever, a matter for praise rather than censure
that Carey's versions so stimulated language
research in India that new versions had to be
made by his successors. It was precisely with
this in mind that Mr. Brandram, Secretary of
the British and Foreign Bible Society, wrote
in 1824 to Serampore concerning the work in
Bible translation:

> You have indeed broken the ice, and given
> the onset, and if you had done nothing more,
> this would of itself afford abundant matter
> for thanksgiving.[4]

Carey was greatly encouraged in his missionary work by the steady growth in the number
of converts and by the increasing number of
baptismal services. This progress was made in
spite of the fact that the requirements for baptism were not, as a general rule, as simple as
in the early years of the mission when usually
all that was required of converts was a profession of faith in Jesus Christ. A probationary
period before baptism was introduced in the
case of all converts concerning whose motives
the missionaries had any doubts. Moreover, at
the time of baptism the questions asked converts became more involved than previously.
Here are a few of the questions put to a Bengali

convert just before his baptism in 1826 and the answers:

Why do you wish to renounce the Hindu religion?

Answer: The Hindu religion enjoins the worship of many gods and proposes various modes of obtaining salvation; these gods I have worshipped, their modes of purification I have observed but all in vain, therefore I wish to renounce it.

Why do you desire to embrace the religion of Jesus Christ?

Answer: Because by embracing it I shall obtain the salvation of my soul.

Do you know that you are a sinner?

Answer: Yes, I know that I am a sinner; I am a great sinner, I have many times broken God's laws.

Without the pardon or removal of sin, can you gain admittance into Heaven?

Answer: No, I cannot, for Heaven is a holy place, and unless I am purified I cannot enter therein.

Has God provided any remedy to take away our sin?

Answer: Yes, God has provided a remedy. He sent the Lord Jesus Christ into the world for the purpose of taking away our sins.[5]

---

[5] Missionary Chronicle, May, 1826.

The question of finding employment for converts who lost their jobs because they became Christians was one which gave Carey and his colleagues much concern. For a number of years the Baptist missionaries had maintained that converts must themselves solve this problem, for the missionaries wished to avoid giving the impression to non-Christians that one sure way to good employment was to become a Christian. In this period, however, Carey began to devise means and ways to help converts. For example, he set up a weaving shop in Serampore to train the children of converts in a useful occupation, and he encouraged Fernandez to establish a paper mill at Dinajpur "with a view of giving employment to the seceders from heathenism." [6]

The most ambitious of Carey's schemes to help converts was undoubtedly the founding of a college for training Indian preachers and teachers. With the tremendous advance taking place in all phases of missionary work, there was great demand for Indian evangelists, preachers and teachers. A prospectus of the college, issued on July 15, 1818 stated that Indian Christians who intended to do missionary work must not only know the doctrine they were to teach but also the doctrines they were

---

[6] Cox, *History of the Baptist Mission*, p. 252.

to combat. To accomplish the first aim, Serampore College proposed to give students a complete course of instruction in Christian theology; to accomplish the second, it proposed to teach Sanskrit and Arabic so that students could thoroughly study the doctrines of Hinduism and Islam.

Entrance to the college was not, however, to be confined to Christian students, but made open to non-Christian students who desired a liberal education.

To house the college, a magnificent building costing £15,000 was erected at Serampore. By 1824 there were fifty-four students in attendance, forty of whom were Christians.

The year 1826 was a historic one for Serampore College, for Dr. Marshman, Carey's colleague, obtained from the king of Denmark a royal charter which gave to the college the right to confer degrees.

Some years later Serampore College decided to undertake the training of Anglo-Indians as missionaries. These men were born in India of European parentage on one side, were accustomed to living in European fashion, were used to the climate of India, and were well acquainted with the language and habits of Indian nationals. Great things were hoped for as a result of the training of Anglo-Indians.

During Carey's lifetime, Serampore College

had four distinguishing features: it was Oriental in character, the main emphasis being laid on the study of Sanskrit rather than English, all lectures being delivered in the vernacular; it was open to Christian students of any religious denomination, and the teaching was strictly nonsectarian; in the college Christian and non-Christian students studied side by side; and finally, the college revealed the growing conception in Carey's mind of the value of concentration rather than diffusion as the policy to be emphasized in missionary work. The last point is important, for at a time when less experienced missionaries connected with other missionary societies were working on the assumption that the evangelization of Bengal and India was their responsibility rather than that of the Indian church, the more experienced Serampore missionaries were expressing the conviction that Indian Christians were the logical persons to evangelize India and that it was the responsibility of missionaries to see that they were efficiently trained for the work.

The distinguishing characteristic of Carey's work was his adoption of the principle of concentration . . . To a far greater degree than any of his predecessors he realized the comparative futility of diffused missions, and the impossibility of converting India by European evangelists. By concentrating the

greater part of his activities within a narrow
circle and by spending his time upon the education and training of Indian teachers he in-
augurated a new method of missionary work
the importance of which it is impossible to
exaggerate.[7]

Although knowledge about non-Christian religions was growing year by year, there is no
indication that Carey in any way changed his
conception of these religions as utterly false
and evil. Carey lived in earnest expectation
that Christianity would triumph over Hinduism; he did not appear to have anticipated that
Christianity would revive Hinduism. Yet this is
exactly what happened. The leader of the
Hindu revival was Rajah Ram Mohun Roy, a
well-educated, learned Brahmin who had acquired a thorough knowledge of Persian, Sanskrit, Arabic, Greek, Latin, and English. He
came into contact with Carey and his colleagues and became acquainted with Christian
doctrine. He then began to study the Vedas in
the light of Christianity, and the result of his
studies led him to believe that he had redis-
covered Christian monotheism in the Vedas.
He thereupon desired "to cleanse Hinduism
from the multiple accretions of latter-day de-

[7] Robinson, *History of Christian Missions*, p. 82.

generacy and to lead it back to the pristine beauty of the Vedic religion." [8]

To this end he established a society which in 1830 came to be known as the Brahmo Samaj. This society embraced hundreds of well-educated and influential Hindus who advocated the philosophical theism of the early Hindu sages and denounced popular superstition. While the society did not repudiate caste, it interpreted caste rules freely. Freytag declares that societies such as the Brahmo Samaj "tried to construct a rationalistic union between Indian, Christian and other religious conceptions." [9] Ram Mohun Roy's interest in Christianity led him to publish *The Precepts of Jesus, the Guide to Happiness and Peace,* in which he praises the teaching of Jesus but questions His divinity and denies the validity of the atonement. Carey's colleague, Marshman, challenged some of the statements in Roy's book, and a controversy arose between them about the deity and atonement of Christ. Marshman attacked Roy's position in a series of articles entitled "A Defense of the Deity and Atonement of Jesus Christ."

The interest of Carey in all matters concerning the welfare of the people of India, non-

---

[8] Richter, *History of Missions in India,* p. 368.
[9] Freytag, *Spiritual Revolution in the East,* p. 139.

Christians and Christians alike, was revealed in many ways during his later years in Serampore. He encouraged Marshman to formulate a plan which would extend the benefits of missionary primary education throughout Bengal and India. Great interest was aroused in this scheme of national education. Courses in the schools were to include arithmetic, geography, history, selections from the Scriptures, selections from Hindu works, and the history of Christianity. Though the teachers were to be non-Christians, their work was to be supervised by missionaries. Forty-five schools were opened in 1817 along the lines of this plan; and in 1819 there were ninety-two schools in the Calcutta area with a total of eight thousand children.

In 1824, however, the Serampore missionaries decided to close all the schools they had opened and operated according to this plan of national education. In order to operate the schools, the missionaries had to make annual appeals to the public for financial assistance. The public responded splendidly, but Carey felt the mission could no longer bear the responsibility which the increasing number of schools entailed. Furthermore he was satisfied that in demonstrating the plan of national education to be workable, the Serampore mission had accomplished its main task and could now leave others to carry on the work it had started.

For a number of years Carey had been conscious of the need for some effective medium by which he and his colleagues could communicate to the public in India their views on pressing social, cultural, and national problems. To remedy this situation, the Serampore mission in 1818 began to publish two magazines and a newspaper. The first magazine, with the title *Dig Darsan* ("The Signpost") was in Bengali and was published monthly and contained articles of general interest. The second periodical, the *Friend of India,* was in English, and was published monthly for two years, quarterly for some years, and eventually weekly until 1883 when it was incorporated with the *Statesman,* a Calcutta newspaper. The *Friend of India* was widely read and was a potent factor in influencing public opinion in India. The third publication, the *Samachar Darpan* ("Mirror of the News") was a Bengali newspaper and had the distinction of being the first newspaper printed in any oriental language. The purpose of this newspaper was "to stimulate a spirit of inquiry and to diffuse information." [10] It was published weekly and ran continuously till 1841.

[10] Marshman, *The Life and Times of Carey, Marshman and Ward,* Vol. II, p. 161.

In 1820 the Serampore missionaries opened a savings bank to encourage thrift among Bengalis, but deposits swelled to such an extent that the bank became too great a burden to the missionaries, and they closed it.

Carey's earnest desire to promote agri-horticultural experiments led him to issue in April, 1820 a *Prospectus of an Agricultural and Horticultural Society,* in which he proposed the formation of an agri-horticultural society. Carey particularly stressed that Indians were to be as eligible as Europeans for membership and for executive positions in the society. The society, which was formally constituted in September of 1820, appointed Indians to the posts of vice-president and joint-secretary.

For many years Carey had protested against the practice of suttee, or widow-burning. His efforts were rewarded when on December 4, 1829, a government regulation declared suttee to be illegal. It was Carey's responsibility, as government translator, to translate this regulation into the vernacular, and so anxious was he to complete the task as speedily as possible that he actually missed the Sunday morning service to do it.

In the early years at Serampore, differences had arisen among the Baptist missionaries because of the refusal of Carey, Marshman, and Ward to admit new missionaries to full partner-

ship in the affairs of the mission. The home
committee of the Baptist Missionary Society
had taken the side of the trio, and had stated
that the management of the mission in Bengal
was to be in the hands of Carey, Marshman,
and Ward for their lifetime. After the death on
May 7, 1815, of Andrew Fuller, secretary of
the B.M.S. from its commencement, a dispute
arose between the Serampore missionaries and
the home committee about exactly the same
matter—the management of the Baptist Mission in Bengal. The dispute was carried on for
several years and became known as the Serampore controversy. The controversy involved
a vital question of mission policy, namely
whether or not missionaries, in managing the
affairs of the Mission in India, were to be
subordinate to the wishes of the committee in
England.

Carey never regarded himself and his colleagues as in a position of subordination to
the officers and members of the Baptist Missionary Society in England, but considered
themselves equal partners with them in a
great enterprise. It was quite out of the question, so far as Carey was concerned, that
the home committee should issue orders to
him. Though Carey received grants from the
society in England, he depended mainly upon
the secular occupations in which he and the

other missionaries engaged to supply money
to finance the work of the mission. He therefore felt free to use the funds of the mission
to purchase property, erect buildings, appoint
Indian evangelists and train missionaries without consulting the home committee. A full account of all decisions reached at Serampore
was sent to the home committee of the B.M.S.
for information, not for approval.

In 1816 the home committee wrote to Carey
of their desire that the Serampore property be
vested in eleven trustees, eight in England and
three in Serampore. When Carey, Marshman,
and Ward made it clear that they were un-
willing to comply with the committee's wishes,
the junior missionaries, all of whom advocated
submission to the home committee in every
matter, withdrew altogether from Serampore
in 1817 and formed a separate Missionary
Union in Calcutta. The argument between the
Serampore missionaries and the home committee over the question of the control of the
mission continued for ten years, and on occasions the exchanges were angry and bitter. The
climax of the controversy was reached in
March, 1827, when it was decided that the
Baptist Missionary Society and the Serampore
Mission were henceforth to operate as separate
and distinct mission organizations.

Richter, the gifted missionary historian, writes about the controversy:

> It was a tragic circumstance that these lives which had ever been "in labours more abundant" should be embittered during a decade and a half by a quarrel of the most petty character with the Society which Carey had himself founded and which really existed on the strength of his success—the Baptist Missionary Society . . . Today we can only read the annals of this unworthy strife with the deepest regret.[11]

It is impossible, however, to escape the feeling that Carey and his colleagues were themselves responsible for bringing about the controversy. It is not enough, as nearly every missionary historian and Carey biographer has done, to consider the controversy in the light of events from the death of Fuller until the 1827 Agreement. The seeds of controversy were sown in 1805 when the Serampore trio refused to admit new missionaries to full and equal partnership in the Baptist Mission at Serampore. The dissatisfaction created among the new missionaries because of this policy spread to their friends in England who were members of the B.M.S. committee. It is argued that the trio did not consider several of the new

---

[11] Richter, *History of Missions in India,* pp. 142, 143.

missionaries as fit to share with them in the management of the Serampore Mission. But if Carey, Marshman and Ward had shown to their junior colleagues that perfect trust which they expected the home committee to have in them, it is doubtful if there would ever have been a controversy.

On the other hand, the committee in England failed fully to appreciate the self-sacrifice which from the very beginning had characterized the lives of Carey, Marshman, and Ward. If they had so chosen, the Serampore trio could have used the large sum of money they earned in secular employment for their own personal benefit rather than devoting all of it to the Baptist Mission. Furthermore, it was too little realized that the contributions which steadily and increasingly flowed into the funds of the Baptist Missionary Society were largely given because of interest in the splendid accomplishments of the Serampore missionaries. If the Serampore missionaries sowed the seeds of controversy, the committee in England, by its lack of sympathetic understanding of all the factors involved and, in some instances, by its tactlessness, helped the controversy to flourish.

There can be little doubt that the very vital question with which the Serampore controversy was concerned, though at times obscured by arguments about property rights, was: To what

extent did the Baptist Missionary Society in
England have the right of control over the
work of its missionaries in India? The principle laid down by Carey and his colleagues
was "Control originates in contribution"; and
since they contributed the major share of the
money required for the Baptist Mission in
Bengal, they reserved the right to control the
work of the mission. The home committee, in
accordance with the same principle, felt that
they should have a share in the control of the
work in the measure that they contributed
financially to it. It is important to realize that
we have here a decided change in missionary
policy as conceived by Carey. The policy under
which he went to India was to make himself
self-supporting as soon as possible and thus re-
lieve the home society of any further financial
responsibility for him. Since the time Carey
went to India, the financial resources of missionary societies had grown to such an extent
that it was no longer deemed necessary to send
missionaries who would be expected to support
themselves by secular employment. It was now
possible for missionaries to devote their whole
time to missionary work under the arrangement that a regular and sufficient salary would
be paid them by the home committee. The missionary whose salary was paid in full from the
homeland came to be regarded as an agent or a

servant of the missionary society rather than
a copartner in a great enterprise. Moreover,
the missionary became dependent on the society at home, not only for his own salary, but
also for the salaries of the nationals whom he
employed and for all the money necessary to
finance local missionary work. The missionary
thus no longer found himself able to appoint
workers or commence new work without first
ascertaining from the home committee if
money was available. All of this meant that
ultimately the control of the work in India
rested with the committee in England.

The agreement of 1827 between the Serampore missionaries and the Baptist Missionary Society brought to an end a bitter controversy, but it also marked the abandonment
of Carey's policy concerning the financial support and the control of missionary work, a
policy which, had it received the encouragement it deserved, might have resulted in a completely self-supporting Bengali church.

Carey's life during the years 1821 to 1834
had its complement of sorrows and joys, of pain
and pleasure, of abuse and honor, of fears and
assurances. The sorrows that came to Carey
were grievous. Carey's second wife, Charlotte,
died in 1821. This well-educated, talented
woman was an invalid for most of the thirteen
years of her marriage, but she made these

years the happiest of Carey's life. Carey said
of Charlotte that she lived first for God, then
for him. The following year Carey's son Felix
died at the early age of thirty-seven. Brilliant
in languages, and skilled in medicine, Felix
had gone in 1807 as a missionary to Burma
with Chater, another Serampore missionary.
Before their departure for Burma, these two
had been given precise instructions by Carey,
among which were these:

> With respect to the Burman language, let
> this occupy your most precious time and your
> most anxious solicitude. Do not be content
> with acquiring this language superficially, but
> make it your own, root and branch. To be-
> come fluent in it, you must attentively listen
> with prying curiosity into the forms of speech,
> the construction and accent of the natives.
> Here all the imitative powers are wanted;
> yet these powers and this attention, without
> continued effort to use all you acquire, and
> as fast as you acquire it, will be compara-
> tively of little use.
>
> As soon as you shall feel your ground well
> in this language, you may compose a gram-
> mar, and also send us some Scripture tracts
> for printing; small and plain, simple Chris-
> tian instruction and Gospel invitation, with-
> out any thing that can irritate the most su-
> perstitious mind.
>
> In prosecuting this work, there are two

things to which especially we would call
your very close attention, viz. the strictest
and most rigid economy, and the cultivation
of brotherly love.

Remember, that the money which you will
expend is neither ours nor yours, for it has
been consecrated to God; and every unnec-
cessary expenditure will be robbing God, and
appropriating to unnecessary secular uses
what is sacred, and consecrated to God and
his cause. In building, especially, remember that you are poor men, and have chosen
a life of poverty and self-denial, with Christ
and his missionary servants. If another person
is profuse in expenditure the consequence is
small, because his property would perhaps
fall into hands where it might be devoted to
the purposes of iniquity; but missionary funds
are in their very circumstances the most
sacred and important of any thing of this
nature on earth.[12]

Felix had put his linguistic and medical tal-
ents to good use in Burma. He translated several of the books of the Bible into Burmese
and some parts of the Buddhist Tripitaka into
English; he prepared a dictionary of Burmese
and Pali words; and he so commended himself
to the king by his medical skill, that the king
appointed him as Burmese ambassador to the
Governor-General of India. This appointment

---

[12] Periodical Accounts, Vol. III, pp. 329, 422.

led Felix to give up missionary work, much to
the great distress of his father, who wrote
"Felix is shrivelled from a missionary into an
ambassador." Some years later Felix realized
how cold his love for the Lord had become,
and in contrition sought God's forgiveness and
restoration to the Serampore fellowship. When
he died in Serampore, he had won back the
confidence of his father and the other missionaries.

In that same year of 1822 the Baptist Mission's first Bengali convert in India, Krishna
Pal, also died in Serampore. Filled with a passion for souls, Krishna Pal spent the years of
his life after his conversion preaching and bap-
tizing throughout Bengal. His death was
keenly felt by Carey.

The first of the Serampore trio to die was
William Ward. He was suddenly taken ill with
cholera one morning in March, 1823, and in a
few hours was dead. The passing of one who
had been a colleague for twenty-three years
was a crushing blow to Carey and Marshman.
Ward was the friendliest one of the trio, and
his warmhearted personality made him the
confidant of all the missionaries' children in
Serampore. It was Ward who, in distress of
heart that Christian friends who had not been
baptized by immersion on profession of faith
were not permitted to take communion in the

Serampore church, persuaded the church to adopt the practice of open communion. At that time he wrote:

> I rejoice that the first Baptist Church in Bengal has shaken off that apparent moroseness of temper which has so long made us appear unlovely in the sight of the Christian world. I am glad that this Church considers real religion alone as the ground of admission to the Lord's table.[13]

Ward was an excellent preacher and an ardent soul-winner. It was his passion for the lost which constrained him regularly to preach at the Lall Bazar Chapel situated in one of Calcutta's neediest areas. It was in the baptistry of the Lall Bazar Chapel that Ward baptized two famous American missionaries, Adoniram and Ann Judson. Like the other members of the Serampore trio, Ward was of scholarly bent, and his great book, *A View of the History, Literature, and Mythology of the Hindoos, including a Minute Description of their Manners and Customs, and Translations from their Principal Works,* published in 1818 was for fifty years the standard work on the subject.

A few months after Ward died, Carey himself nearly died. He was returning from Cal-

---

[13] Marshman, *The Life and Labours of Carey, Marshman and Ward,* p. 83.

cutta by boat, and as he stepped ashore at
Serampore he slipped and fell, severely injur-
ing his hip. A few days later his temperature
rose so alarmingly it was feared he could not
possibly survive. He did recover, but for six
months he could not walk without the help of
crutches.

At no time in his missionary career did
Carey experience such financial problems as he
had to face in the last years of his life at Serampore. Some of these problems he himself
created. Disregarding the advice of his colleagues, Carey sometimes pushed ahead with
the publication of new translations when there
were not sufficient funds in the translation account to meet the cost. This forced the missionaries to borrow heavily from time to time, and
at a high rate of interest. Carey also found it
difficult to refuse any request to station a missionary in a new area, even when this involved
expenditure beyond the financial resources of
the mission. At times he sorely tried his colleagues when his enthusiasm for establishing
new mission stations appeared to them to ex-
ceed the bounds of prudence.

In 1830 the Indian Administration, which
was facing a serious deficit, decided to take
certain measures in the interests of economy,
and two of these decisions had serious financial
repercussions on Carey and the Serampore

Mission: the College of Fort William professorships were abolished, and Carey was given a pension of half salary, namely 500 rupees a month; and the post of Bengali translator to the government which Carey had held for eight years at 300 rupees a month was suspended. When the Serampore brotherhood met to consider the implications of this drop in income of 800 rupees a month and to pray about it, Carey and Marshman wept as they entreated God not to forsake them in their old age. Carey was particularly concerned about the mission stations of the Serampore Mission, for he had been contributing 600 rupees monthly to them from his salary. Full reports setting forth the gravity of the crisis were sent to the Honorary Secretary and Treasurer of the Serampore Mission in England, Mr. Samuel Hope of Liverpool, and to the Rev. Christopher Anderson, the gifted minister of Charlotte Baptist Chapel, Edinburgh, Scotland. These two launched an appeal for Serampore which met with a generous response from Christians in Scotland and England. Carey was overjoyed at this manifestation of love and of confidence in him and his colleagues.

Three years later Anderson and Hope had to issue an emergent appeal for yet another financial exigency at Serampore. During the years 1830-1833 Calcutta had a series of finan-

cial crises when, one by one, six of India's leading mercantile and banking firms failed for a
total amount of £16,000,000. Two of these
firms, Alexander and Company and Mackin-
tosh and Company, were the Serampore mission
bankers, and their failure meant the total loss
of the Mission's invested funds, which included
Fernandez' legacy of £1,600 for Dinajpur, the
Delhi School Fund of £800 and the Jessore
School's Fund of £720; it also meant the entire loss of funds which Carey and Marshman,
with the permission of the Serampore Brotherhood, had been setting aside for their old age.
This sorry situation was further complicated
by the fact that no bank in Calcutta was willing to lend money to the Serampore missionaries to tide them over the crisis. Unexpected
help came from one of Carey's former students
in the College of Fort William, Mr. Garrett,
who pledged his own credit with the Bank of
Bengal to secure a loan for Carey and the
Serampore mission. This made it possible for
the various mission stations to remain in operation until specially raised funds arrived from
Anderson and Hope in Great Britain.

The joys that Carey experienced in the last
period of his life were abundant, and in his
diaries and letters ascriptions of praise to God
for His blessings are repeatedly recorded. Two
years after the death of his second wife, Char-

lotte, Carey married a widow, Grace Hughes, who, though unable to give him the intellectual stimulus he had enjoyed in his second marriage, lavished a wealth of care and affection upon him and wonderfully nursed him during his spells of illness and infirmity.

Carey's surviving sons, Jonathan, a Calcutta Supreme Court attorney, and Jabez and William, who were missionaries, all lived near enough to Serampore to make frequent visits with their families. Carey took great pride in his children and grandchildren, and rejoiced in their loyalty to Christ. Their presence greatly cheered him in his old age.

It was a constant source of gratification to Carey that through the work of the Serampore mission the number of Indian converts steadily increased, that into the hands of such converts could be placed the Scriptures in their own languages, and that promising converts could receive an excellent training for the ministry at Serampore College.

Carey's wide interests were recognized when in 1823 he was honored by three British societies. The Royal Horticultural Society of London and the Geological Society elected him to membership, and the Linnean Society made him a Fellow.

To the end of his life, Carey maintained keen interest in horticulture. After his death,

when the members of the agri-horticultural
society decided to honor him, their founder,
they adopted the following resolution:

> That the Agricultural and Horticultural So-
> ciety of India, duly estimating the great and
> important services rendered to the interest of
> British India by the founder of the institu-
> tion, the late Reverend Dr. William Carey,
> who unceasingly applied his great talents,
> abilities, and influence in advancing the hap-
> piness of India—more especially by the
> spread of an improved system of husbandry
> and gardening—desire to mark, by some
> permanent record, their sense of his tran-
> scendent worth, by placing a marble bust to
> his memory in the Society's new apartments
> at the Metcalfe Hall, there to remain a last-
> ing testimony to the pure and disinterested
> zeal and labours of so illustrious a character:
> that a subscription, accordingly, from among
> the members of the Society, be urgently rec-
> ommended for the accomplishment of the
> above object.

Carey's pride in Serampore College was un-
bounded. He was proud of the magnificent
college building, which was Ionic in design
and was for many years considered the finest of
its kind in India. The edifice was planned by
Major Wickedie of the Danish government
and incorporated suggestions made by the
Governor-General of India, who took great

interest in the scheme. The two lovely cast-iron, brass-pillared staircases in the college building were made in Birmingham, England. The gate at the main entrance to the college was also made in Birmingham. Carey took the greatest pride in the students who attended Serampore and to whom he lectured as professor of divinity and lecturer in botany and zoology. One of the final acts of Carey's life was to formulate the statutes of the college, and this he did in consultation with Marshman and Marshman's son, John. These statutes emphasize Carey's loyalty to historic Christianity and at the same time clearly show the catholicity of his spirit. The statutes required all members of the college council and faculty to be believers in the deity and atonement of Jesus Christ; but the statutes also permitted one member of the college council of five to be other than a Baptist, and opened the college to all, irrespective of creed, color, caste or race. After Carey's death the college continued until 1883, when it was replaced by an Indian Training Institute. The college was reorganized in 1910, and became a union institution in 1918. Today Serampore College teaches the arts, science and theology, and is the only recognized institution in India to grant degrees in theology. The Theological University functions of Serampore College are administered by the college senate on behalf of twenty affiliated colleges in India.

To the Baptist Mission at Serampore there came in the last years of Carey's life a steady stream of visitors to see him, to talk with him and, in many instances, to secure his counsel, even his blessing. These visitors included prominent Indian leaders, high government officials, Anglican bishops and chaplains, civilian and military officers, scholars, missionary statesmen and missionaries of different denominations. One of the most famous of the last-named was Alexander Duff, missionary of the Church of Scotland, who talked encouragingly to Carey as he lay on his deathbed, and reminded him of his notable achievements as a missionary. Carey whispered to him, "Mr. Duff, you have been speaking about Dr. Carey, Dr. Carey; when I am gone, say nothing about Dr. Carey—speak about Dr. Carey's Saviour."

In 1832, at the age of seventy-one, Carey still engaged regularly in preaching, lecturing and translating the Scriptures, but the following year he took seriously ill on several occasions and had to give up all work. For the last months of his life he was confined to bed. He died on Monday afternoon, June 9, 1843, and was buried the following morning in the Baptist Mission Cemetery, Serampore. The streets of Serampore were lined with spectators as the coffin was carried to the cemetery. Among those attending the funeral were the Danish Governor of Serampore, members of the Governor's Council, and an official representative of the Governor-General of India. The sermon at the grave was preached by Marshman. In keeping with his wishes, Carey was buried beside his second wife, Charlotte; and on the same memorial stone which recorded her death were inscribed the words which Carey had himself selected:

William Carey

Born August 17, 1761,   Died June 1834

"A wretched, poor and helpless worm,
On Thy kind arms I fall."

How characteristic of Carey to proclaim in death, as in life, his utter dependence on the goodness and mercy of God. But it was not alone this spirit of dependence upon God which made Carey great. The significance of Carey lies in his apprehension of the corresponding truth of God's dependence upon His people. The Christians of Carey's day looked to God to bring about the conversion of the heathen and left the task entirely to Him. Carey made it clear that God was looking to them to evangelize the world—that the conversion of the world to Christ is not accomplished by God alone but by God and His Church.

Carey enunciated this great truth in sermons and in his "Enquiry," and he also proved it by his own missionary career. He was proud to be a missionary of Jesus Christ to foreign lands. On one occasion he wrote:

> I feel myself perfectly at home in my work as a missionary, and rejoice that God has given me this great favour to "preach among the Gentiles the unsearchable riches of Christ." I would not change my station for all the society in England, much as I prize it; nor indeed for all the wealth in the world. May I but be useful in laying the foundation of the Church of Christ in India. I desire no greater reward, and can receive no higher honour.[14]

Though Carey did not seek fame, he died a famous man. The self-sacrificial system he devised according to which he and his colleagues lived as a missionary community in Serampore and pooled all their earnings for missionary work captured the imagination of the Christian public throughout the world and made the name of Carey a household word. Carey's brilliance in numerous languages won for him the respect of scholars in many lands and he received tributes such as that of the celebrated lexicographer Ram Kamal Sen who wrote:

Whatever has been done towards the revival

---

[14] *Periodical Accounts,* Vol. I, p. 491.

of the Bengali language, its improvement, and in fact, the establishment of it as a language, must be attributed to that excellent man, Dr. Carey, and his colleagues, by whose liberality and great exertions, many works have been carried through the press, and the general tone of the language of this province has been greatly raised.[15]

The establishment of Serampore College for the training of Indian Christian nationals in the realization that ultimately the task of evangelizing India would be that of nationals rather than European missionaries revealed Carey's keen foresight in missionary policy and earned for him everywhere the praise of students of missions. Carey's emphasis upon a deep concern for souls, upon the need for each missionary to engage devotedly in soul-winning, and upon preaching Christ as God's only provision for the sins of the world, commended him to evangelical Christians in every land. Above all, Carey is famous because at a time in the history of the Church when Christians were almost completely ignoring their responsibility to preach the Gospel to every creature, he, by organizing a foreign missionary society and by going as a missionary, roused the whole Protestant Christian world to a sense of its obligation to non-Christians. The Baptist

---

[15] Sen, *Bengali-English Dictionary* (Preface).

Missionary Society was organized by Carey in 1792. In the years that followed, inspired by Carey's noble example, other great churches and denominations throughout the world established foreign missionary organizations. Thus to William Carey, in the providence of God, belongs the honor of being the Father of Modern Missions.

Appendix A

The Serampore Form of Agreement

Form of Agreement respecting the great principles upon which the Brethren of the Mission at Serampore think it their duty to act in the work of instructing the Heathen, agreed upon at a meeting of the Brethren at Serampore, on Monday, October 7, 1805.

The Redeemer, in planting us in this heathen nation, rather than in any other, has imposed upon us the cultivation of peculiar qualifications. We are firmly persuaded that Paul might plant and Apollos water, in vain, in any part of the world, did not God give the increase. We are sure that only those who are ordained to eternal life will believe, and that God alone can add to the Church such as shall be saved. Nevertheless we cannot but observe with admiration that Paul, the great champion for the glorious doctrines of free and sovereign grace, was the most conspicuous for his personal zeal in the work of persuading men to be reconciled to God. In this respect he is a noble example for our imitation. Our Lord intimated to those of His apostles who were fishermen, that he would make them fishers of men, intimating that in all weathers, and amidst every disappointment, they were to aim at drawing men to the shores of eternal life. Solomon says, "He that winneth souls is wise," implying, no doubt, that the work of gaining over men to the side of God was to be done by winning methods, and that it required the greatest wisdom to do it with success. Upon these points, we think it right to fix our serious and abiding attention.

1. In order to be prepared for our great and solemn work, it is absolutely necessary that we set an infinite value upon immortal souls; that we often endeavour to affect our minds with the dreadful loss sustained by an unconverted soul launched into eternity. It becomes us to fix in our minds the awful doctrine of eternal punishment, and to realise frequently the inconceivably awful condition of this vast country, lying in the arms of the wicked one. If we have not this awful sense of the value of souls, it is impossible that we can feel aright in any other part of our work, and in this case

it had been better for us to have been in any
other situation rather than in that of a missionary. Oh! may our hearts bleed over these poor
idolators and may their case lie with continued
weight on our minds, that we may resemble
that eminent Missionary, who compared the
travail of his soul, on account of the spiritual
state of those committed to his charge, to the
pains of childbirth. But while we thus mourn
over their miserable condition, we should not
be discouraged, as though their recovery were
impossible. He who raised the sottish and
brutalised Britons to sit in heavenly places in
Christ Jesus, can raise these slaves of superstition, purify their hearts by faith, and make
them worshippers of the one God in spirit and
in truth. The promises are fully sufficient to
remove our doubts, and to make us anticipate
that not very distant period when He will famish all the gods of India, and cause these very
idolaters to cast their idols to the moles and to
the bats, and renounce for ever the work of
their own hands.

2. It is very important that we should gain all
the information we can of the snares and de-
lusions in which these heathen are held. By this
means we shall be able to converse with them
in an intelligible manner. To know their modes
of thinking, their habits, their propensities,
their antipathies, the way in which they reason

about God, sin, holiness, the way of salvation, and a future state, to be aware of the bewitching nature of their idolatrous worship, feasts, songs, etc., is of the highest consequence, if we would gain their attention to our discourse, and would avoid being barbarians to them. This knowledge may be easily obtained by conversing with sensible natives, by reading some parts of their works and by attentively observing their manners and customs.

3. It is necessary, in our intercourse with the Hindoos, that, as far as we are able, we abstain from those things which would increase their prejudices against the Gospel. Those parts of English manners which are most offensive to them should be kept out of sight as much as possible. We should also avoid every degree of cruelty to animals. Nor is it advisable at once to attack their prejudices by exhibiting with acrimony the sins of their gods; neither should we on any account do violence to their images, nor interrupt their worship. The real conquests of the Gospel are those of love: "And I, if I be lifted up, will draw all men unto me." In this respect, let us be continually fearful lest one unguarded word, or one unnecessary display of the difference betwixt us, in manners, etc., should set the natives at a greater distance from us. Paul's readiness to become all things to all men, that he might by

any means save some and his disposition to abstain even from necessary comforts that he might not offend the weak, are circumstances worthy of our particular notice. This line of conduct we may be sure was founded on the wisest principles. Placed amidst a people very much like the hearers of the Apostle, in many respects, we may now perceive the solid wisdom which guided him as a missionary. The mild manners of the Moravians, and also of the Quakers, towards the North American Indians, have, in many instances, gained the affections and confidence of heathens in a wonderful manner. He who is too proud to stoop to others in order to draw them to him, though he may know that they are in many respects inferior to himself, is ill-qualified to become a Missionary. The words of a most successful preacher of the Gospel still living, "that he would not care if the people trampled him under their feet, if he might become useful to their souls", are expressive of the very temper we should always cultivate.

4. It becomes us to watch all opportunities of doing good. A missionary would be highly culpable if he contented himself with preaching two or three times a week to those persons whom he might be able to get together into a place of worship. To carry on conversations with the natives almost every hour in the day,

to go from village to village, from market to market, from one assembly to another, to talk to servants, labourers, etc., as often as opportunity offers, and to be instant in season and out of season, this is the life to which we are called in this country. We are apt to relax in these active exertions especially in a warm climate: but we shall do well always to fix in our minds that life is short, that all around us are perishing, and that we incur a dreadful woe if we proclaim not the glad tiding of salvation.

5. In preaching to the heathen, we must keep to the example of Paul, and make the great subject of our preaching, Christ the Crucified. It would be very easy for a missionary to preach nothing but truths, and that for many years together, without any well-grounded hope of becoming useful to one soul. The doctrine of Christ's expiatory death and all-sufficient merits has been, and must ever remain, the grand mean of conversion. This doctrine, and others immediately connected with it, have constantly nourished and sanctified the Church. Oh that these glorious truths may ever be the joy and strength of our own souls and then they will not fail to become the matter of our conversation to others. It was the proclaiming of these doctrines that made the Reformation from Popery in the time of Luther spread with such rapidity. It was these

truths that filled the sermons of the modern apostles, Whitefield, Wesley, etc., when the light of the Gospel which had been held up with such glorious effects by the Puritans was almost extinguished in England. It is a well-known fact that the most successful missionaries in the world at the present day make the atonement of Christ their continued theme. We mean the Moravians. They attribute all their success to the preaching of the death of our Saviour. So far as our experience goes in this work, we must freely acknowledge that every Hindoo among us who has been gained to Christ, has been won by the astonishing and all-constraining love exhibited in our Redeemer's propitiatory death. O then may we resolve to know nothing among Hindoos and Mussulmans but Christ and Him crucified.

6. It is absolutely necessary that the natives should have an entire confidence in us, and feel quite at home in our company. To gain this confidence we must on all occasions be willing to hear their complaints: we must give them the kindest advice: and we must decide upon everything brought before us in the most open, upright, and impartial manner. We ought to be easy of access, to condescend to them as much as possible, and on all occasions to treat them as our equals. All passionate behaviour will sink our characters exceedingly in their

estimation. All force, and everything haughty, reserved and forbidding, it becomes us ever to shun with the greatest care. We can never make sacrifices too great, when the eternal salvation of souls is the object except, indeed, we sacrifice the commands of Christ.

7. Another important part of our work is to build up, and watch over, the souls that may be gathered. In this work we shall do well to simplify our first instructions as much as possible, and to press the great principles of the Gospel upon the minds of the converts till they be thoroughly settled and grounded in the foundation of their hope towards God. We must be willing to spend some time with them daily, if possible, in this work. We must have much patience with them, though they may grow very slowly in divine knowledge. We ought also to endeavour as much as possible to form them to habits of industry, and assist them in procuring such employments as may be pursued with the least danger of temptations to evil. Here too we shall have occasion to exercise much tenderness and forbearance, knowing that industrious habits are formed with difficulty by all heathen nations.

We ought also to remember that these persons have made no common sacrifices in renouncing their connections, their homes, their former situations and means of support, and that it will be very difficult for them to procure employment with heathen masters. In these circumstances, if we do not sympathise with them in their temporal losses for Christ, we shall be guilty of great cruelty.

As we consider it our duty to honour the civil magistrate, and in every state and country to render him the readiest obedience, whether we be persecuted or protected, it becomes us to instruct our native brethren in the same principles. A sense of gratitude too presses this obligation upon us in a peculiar manner in return for the liberal protection we have experienced. It is equally our wisdom and our duty also to show to the civil power, that it has nothing to fear from the progress of Missions, since a real follower of Christ must resist the example of his great Master, and all the precepts the Bible contains on this subject, before he can become disloyal. Converted heathens, being brought over to the religion of their Christian Governors, if duly instructed, are much more likely to love them, and be united to them, than subjects of a different religion.

To bear the faults of our native brethren, so as to reprove them with tenderness, and set them right in the necessity of a holy conversation, is a very necessary duty. We should remember the gross darkness in which they were so lately involved, having never had any just and adequate ideas of the evil of sin or its consequences. We should also recollect how backward human nature is in forming spiritual ideas, and entering upon a holy self-denying conversation. We ought not, therefore, even after many falls, to give up and cast away a relapsed convert while he manifests the least inclination to be washed from his filthiness.

In walking before native converts, much care and circumspection are absolutely necessary. The falls of Christians in Europe have not such a fatal tendency as they must have in this country, because there the Word of God always commands more attention than the conduct of the most exalted Christian. But here those around us, in consequence of their little knowledge of the Scriptures, must necessarily take our conduct as a specimen of what Christ looks for in His disciples. They know only the Saviour and His doctrine as they shine forth in us.

In conversing with the wives of native converts, and leading them on in the ways of Christ, so that they may be an ornament to the Christian cause, and make known the Gospel to the native women, we hope always to have the assistance of the females who have embarked with us in the Mission. We see that in primitive times the Apostles were very much assisted in their great work by several pious females. The great value of female help may easily be appreciated if we consider how much the Asiatic women are shut up from the men, and especially from men of another caste. It behooves us therefore, to afford to our European sisters all possible assistance in acquiring the language, that they may, in every way which Providence may open to them, become instrumental in promoting the salvation of the millions of native women who are in a great measure excluded from all opportunities of hearing the Word from the mouths of European missionaries. A European sister may do much for the cause in this respect, by promoting the holiness, and stirring up the zeal, of the female native converts. A real missionary becomes in a sense a father to his people. If he feel all the anxiety and tender solicitude of a father, all that delight in their welfare and company that a father does in the midst of his children, they will feel all that freedom with, and confidence in him which he can desire. He will be wholly unable to lead them on in a regular and happy manner, unless they can be induced to open their minds to him, and unless a sincere and mutual esteem subsist on both sides.

8. Another part of our work is the forming of our native brethren to usefulness, fostering every kind of genius, and cherishing every gift

and grace in them. In this respect we can scarcely be too lavish of our attention to their improvement. It is only by means of native preachers that we can hope for the universal spread of the Gospel throughout this immense continent. Europeans are too few, and their subsistence costs too much for us ever to hope that they can possibly be the instruments of the universal diffusion of the Word amongst so many millions of souls spread over such a large portion of the habitable globe. Their incapability of bearing the intense heat of the climate in perpetual itineracies, and the heavy expenses of their journeys, not to say anything of the prejudices of the natives against the very presence of Europeans, and the great difficulty of becoming fluent in their languages, render it an absolute duty to cherish native gifts, and to send forth as many native preachers as possible. If the practice of confining the ministry of the Word to a single individual in a Church be once established amongst us, we despair of the Gospel's ever making much progress in India by our means. Let us therefore use every gift, and continually urge on our native brethren to press upon their countrymen the glorious Gospel of the blessed God.

Still further to strengthen the cause of Christ in this country, and as far as in our power, to give it a permanent establishment, even when

the efforts of Europeans may fail, we think it
our duty, as soon as possible, to advise the
native brethren who may be formed into separate Churches to choose their pastors and
deacons from amongst their own countrymen,
that the Word may be statedly preached, and
the ordinances of Christ administered, in each
Church by the native minister, as much as
possible without the interference of the missionary of the district who will constantly superin-
tend their affairs, give them advice in cases of
order and discipline, and correct any errors
into which they may fall, and who joying and
beholding their order, and the steadfastness of
their faith in Christ, may direct his efforts continually to the planting of new Churches in
other places, and to the spread of the Gospel
throughout his district as much as in his power.
By this means the unity of the missionary character will be preserved, all the missionaries will
still form one body, each one moveable as the
good of the cause may require; the different
native Churches will also naturally learn to
care and provide for their ministers, for their
Church expenses, the raising of places of worship, etc., and the whole administration will
assume a native aspect; by which means the
inhabitants will more readily identify the cause
as belonging to their own nation, and their
prejudices at falling into the hands of Euro-

peans will entirely vanish. It may be hoped
too that the pastors of these Churches, and the
members in general, will feel a new energy in
attempting to spread the Gospel, when they
shall thus freely enjoy the privileges of the
Gospel amongst themselves. Under the divine
blessing, if in the course of a few years a number of native Churches be thus established,
from them the Word of God may sound out
even to the extremities of India; and numbers
of preachers being raised up and sent forth,
may form a body of native missionaries, inured
to the climate, acquainted with the customs,
language, modes of speech, and reasoning of
the inhabitants; able to become perfectly fa-
miliar with them, to enter their houses, to live
upon their food, to sleep with them, or under a
tree; and who may travel from one end of the
country to the other almost without any expense. These Churches will be in no immediate
danger of falling into errors or disorders, because the whole of their affairs will be constantly superintended by a European missionary. The advantages of this plan are so evident,
that to carry it into complete effect ought to be
our continued concern. That we may discharge
the important obligations of watching over
these infant churches when formed, and of urging them to maintain a steady discipline, to
hold forth the clear and cheering light of evan-

gelical truth in this region and shadow of death, and to walk in all respects as those who have been called out of darkness into marvellous light, we should go continually to the Source of all grace and strength; for if, to become the shepherd of one Church be a most solemn and weighty charge, what must it be to watch over a number of Churches just raised from a state of heathenism, and placed at a distance from each other.

We have thought it our duty not to change the names of native converts, observing from Scripture that the Apostles did not change those of the first Christians turned from heathenism, as the names Epaphroditus, Phebe, Fortunatus, Sylvanus, Apollos, Hermes, Junia, Narcissus, etc., prove. Almost all these names are derived from those of heathen gods. We think the great object which divine Providence has in view in causing the Gospel to be promulgated in the world, is not the changing of the names, the dress, the food, and the innocent usages of mankind, but to produce a moral and divine change in the hearts and conduct of men. It would not be right to perpetuate the names of heathen gods amongst Christians; neither is it necessary or prudent to give a new name to every man after his conversion, as hereby the economy of families, neighbourhoods, etc., would be needlessly dis-

turbed. In other respects we think it our duty
to lead our brethren by example, by mild per-
suasion, and by opening and illuminating their
minds in a gradual way, rather than use au-
thoritative means. By this they learn to see the
evil of a custom, and then to despise and forsake it; whereas in cases where force is used,
though they may leave off that which is wrong
while in our presence, yet not having seen the
evil of it, they are in danger of using hypocrisy,
and of doing that out of our presence which
they dare not do in it.

9. It becomes us also to labour with all our
might in forwarding translations of the sacred
Scriptures in the languages of Hindoostan. The
help which God has already afforded us in this
work is a loud call to us to "go forward." So
far, therefore, as God has qualified us to learn
those languages which are necessary, we consider it our bounden duty to apply with un-
wearied assiduity in acquiring them. We consider the publication of the divine Word
throughout India as an object which we ought
never to give up till accomplished, looking to
the Fountain of all knowledge and strength,
to qualify us for this great work, and to carry
us through it to the praise of His holy name.

It becomes us to use all assiduity in explain-
ing and distributing the divine Word on all occasions, and by every means in our power to

excite the attention and reverence of the natives towards it, as the fountain of eternal truth, and the message of salvation to men. It is our duty also to distribute, as extensively as possible, the different religious tracts which are published. Considering how much the general diffusion of the knowledge of Christ depends upon a constant and liberal distribution of the Word, and of these tracts all over the country, we should keep this continually in mind, and watch all opportunities of putting even single tracts into the hands of those persons with whom we occasionally meet. We should endeavour to ascertain where large assemblies of natives are to be found, that we may attend upon them, and gladden whole villages at once with the tidings of salvation.

The establishment of native free schools is also an object highly important to the future conquests of the Gospel. Of this very pleasing and interesting part of our missionary labours we should endeavour not to be unmindful. As opportunities are afforded, it becomes us to establish, visit, and encourage these institutions, and to recommend the establishment of them to other Europeans. The progress of divine light is gradual, both as it respects individuals and nations. Whatever therefore tends to increase the body of holy light in these dark regions, is as bread cast upon the waters, to be seen after many days. In many ways the progress of providential events is preparing the Hindoos for casting their idols to the moles and the bats, and for becoming a part of the chosen generation, the royal priesthood, the holy nation. Some parts of missionary labours very properly tend to the present conversion of the heathen, and others to the ushering in of the glorious period when a nation shall be born in a day. Of the latter are native free schools.

10. That which, as a means, is to fit us for the discharge of these laborious and unutterably important labours, is the being instant in prayer, and the cultivation of personal religion. Let us ever have in remembrance the examples of those who have been most eminent in the work of God. Let us often look at Brainerd in the woods of America, pouring out his very soul before God for the perishing heathen, without whose salvation nothing could make him happy. Prayer, secret, fervent, believing prayer, lies at the root of all personal godliness. A competent knowledge of the languages where a missionary lives, a mild and winning temper, and a heart given up to God in closest religion, these, these are the attainments which, more than all knowledge or all other gifts, will fit us to become the instruments of God in the great work of human redemption. Let us then ever be united in prayer at stated

seasons, whatever distance may separate us, and let each one of us lay it upon his heart that we will seek to be fervent in spirit, wrestling with God, till He famish these idols, and cause the heathen to experience the blessedness that is in Christ. Finally. Let us give ourselves unreservedly to this glorious cause. Let us never think that our time, our gifts, our strength, our families, or even the clothes we wear, are our own. Let us sanctify them all to God and His cause. Oh that He may sanctify us for His work. Let us for ever shut out the idea of laying up a cowrie for ourselves or our children. If we give up the resolution which was formed on the subject of private trade when we first united at Serampore, the Mission is from that hour a lost cause. A worldly spirit, quarrels, and every evil work will succeed the moment it is admitted that each brother may do something on his own account. Woe to that man who shall ever make the smallest movement toward such a measure! Let us continually watch against a worldly spirit, and cultivate a Christian indifference towards every indulgence. Rather let us bear hardness as good soldiers of Jesus Christ and endeavour to learn in every state to be content.

If in this way we are enabled to glorify God with our bodies and spirits which are His, our wants will be His care. No private family ever enjoyed a greater portion of happiness, even in the most prosperous gale of worldly prosperity, than we have done since we resolved to have all things in common and that no one should pursue business for his own exclusive advantage. If we are enabled to persevere in the same principles, we may hope that multitudes of converted souls will have reason to bless God to all eternity for sending His Gospel into this country.

To keep these ideas alive in our minds, we resolve that this agreement shall be read publicly, at every station, at our three annual meetings, viz. on the first Lord's day in January, in May and October.

WILLIAM CAREY	JOHN BLISS
JOSHUA MARSHMAN	WILLIAM MOORE
WILLIAM WARD	JOSHUA ROWE
JOHN CHAMBERLAIN	FELIX CAREY
RICHARD MARDON	

MISSION HOUSE, SERAMPORE.

Appendix B

Charter of Incorporation of Serampore College

We, Frederick the Sixth, by the Grace of God King of Denmark, the Venders and Gothers, Duke of Slesvig Holsten, Stormarn, Ditmarsken, Limessborg and Oldenborg, by writings these make known and publicly declare, that whereas William Carey and Joshua Marshman, Doctors of Divinity, and John Clark Marshman, Esq., inhabitants of our town of Fredericksnagore (or Serampore) in Bengal, being desirous of founding a College to promote piety and learning particularly among the native Christian population of India, have to secure this object erected suitable buildings and purchased and collected suitable books, maps, etc., and have humbly besought us to grant unto them and such persons as shall be elected by them and their successors to form the Council of the College in the manner to be hereafter named, our Royal Charter of Incorporation that they may the more effectually carry into execution the purposes abovementioned:—We, being desirous to encourage so laudable an undertaking, have of our special grace and free motion, ordained, constituted, granted and declared, and by the presents We do for ourselves, our heirs and successors ordain, constitute, grant and declare:

1. That the said William Carey, Joshua Marshman and John Clark Marshman, and such other person or persons as shall successively be elected and appointed to the Council of the said College, in the manner hereafter mentioned, shall by virtue of the presents be for ever hereafter one body politic and incorporate by the name of the Serampore College for the purposes aforesaid to have perpetual succession and to have a common seal, and by the said name to sue and be sued, to implead and be impleaded, and to answer and be answered unto in every court and place belonging to us, our heirs and successors.

2. And We do hereby ordain, constitute and declare that the persons hereby incorporated and their successors shall for ever be competent in law to purchase, hold and enjoy for them and their successors any goods and chattels whatsoever and to receive, purchase, hold

and enjoy, they and their successors, any lands, tenements or hereditaments whatever and that they shall have full power and authority to sell, exchange or otherwise dispose of any real or personal property to be by them acquired as aforesaid, unless the sale or alienation of such property be specially prohibited by the donor or donors thereof, and to do all things relating to the said College or Corporation in as ample a manner or form as any of our liege subjects, or any other body politic or corporate in our said kingdom or its dependencies may or can do.

3. And We do hereby ordain, grant and declare that the number of Professors, Fellows or Student Tutors and Students, shall be indefinite and that the said William Carey, Joshua Marshman and John Clark Marshman, shall be the first Council of the said College, and that in the event of its appearing to them necessary during their lifetime, or in the case of the death of any one of the three members of the said first Council, the survivors or survivor shall and may under their respective hands and seals appoint such other person or persons to be members of the said first Council, the survivors or survivor shall and may under their respective hands and seals appoint such other person or persons to be members of the Council of the College, and to succeed each other

so as to become members of the said Council
in the order in which they shall be appointed,
to the intent that the Council of the said College shall for ever consist of at least three persons.

4. And We do hereby further ordain, grant
and declare, that for the better government of
the said College, and the better management
of its concerns, the said William Carey,
Joshua Marshman and John Clark Marshman,
the members of the first Council, shall have
full power and authority for the space of ten
years from the date of these presents, to make
and establish such statutes as shall appear to
them useful and necessary for the government
of the said College, in which statutes they shall
define the powers to be entrusted to their successors, to the Professors, the Fellows or Student Tutors, and the other Officers thereof,
and the duties to be performed by these re-
spectively for the management of the estates,
lands, revenues and goods—and of the business of the said College, and the manner of
proposing, electing, admitting and removing
all and every one of the Council, the Professors, the Fellows or Tutors, the officers, the
students and the servants thereof, and shall
make and establish generally all such other
statutes as may appear to them necessary for
the future good government and prosperity of

the said College, provided that these statutes be not contrary to the laws and statutes of our realm.

5. And We do hereby further ordain, grant and declare, that the statutes thus made and established by the said three members of the first Council, and given or left in writing under their respective hands, shall be valid and in full force at the expiration of ten years from the date of these presents, so that no future Council of the College shall have power to alter, change or vary them in any manner whatever and that the statutes shall for ever be considered the constitution of the said College. And We do hereby appoint and declare that these statutes shall be made and established by the said William Carey, Joshua Marshman and John Clark Marshman alone, so that in case either of them should die before the expiration of ten years, the power of completing or perfecting these statutes shall devolve wholly on the survivors or survivor; and that in case all three of them should die before the expiration of ten years, the statutes which they have left in writing under their hands, or under the hand of the last survivor among them shall be considered "The Fundamental Statutes and Constitution of Serampore College," incapable of receiving either addition or alteration, and shall and may be registered in

our Royal Court of Chancery as "The Statutes
and Constitution of Serampore College."

6. And we do hereby further appoint, grant
and declare that from and after the completion
of the statutes of the said College in the above
said time of ten years, the said Council of the
College shall be deemed to consist of a Master
or President and two or four members who
may be Professors or otherwise as the statutes
may direct so that the said Council shall not
contain less than three, nor more than five
persons, as shall be defined in the statutes. The
Council shall ever be elected as the Statutes of
the College may direct, yet the said Master or
President shall always previously have been a
Member of the said College; and upon the
decease of the said Master or President, the
Council of the said College shall be unable to
do any act or deed until the appointment of a
new Master or President save and except the
appointment of such a Master.

7. And we further appoint, grant and declare, that the said William Carey, Joshua
Marshman and John Clark Marshman, the
members of the first Council, and their successors for ever, shall have the power of conferring upon the students of the said College,
Native Christians as well as others, degrees of
rank and honour according to their proficiency
in as ample a manner as any other such Col-

lege, yet the said Serampore College shall only
have the power of conferring such degrees on
the students that testify their proficiency in
Science and no rank or other special right shall
be connected therewith in our dominions. And
We do hereby further appoint, grant and declare, that after the expiration of the said ten
years, the said Council of the College and their
successors for ever shall have power to make
and establish such orders and by-laws as shall
appear to them useful and necessary for the
government of the said College, and to alter,
suspend or repeal those already made, and
from time to time make such new ones in their
room as shall appear to them most proper and
expedient provided the same be not repugnant
to the Statutes of the College, or to the laws of
our realm, and that after the expiration of
these ten years any member of the Council
shall have power to move the enactment of any
new by-law, or the alteration, suspension or
repeal of any existing one provided notice of
such motion shall have been delivered in writing to the Master and read from the Chair at
one previous meeting of the Council of the said
College, but that no such motion shall be
deemed to have passed in the affirmative, until
the same shall have been discussed and decided by ballot at another meeting summoned
especially for that purpose, a majority of the

members then present having voted in the affirmative; and in this, as in all other cases, if the votes be equal, the master or the President shall have the casting vote.

Given at our Royal Palace at Copenhagen on the twenty-third day of February, in the year of our Lord one thousand, eight hundred and twenty-seven, in the nineteenth year of our reign.

Under our Royal Hand and Seal
FREDERICK R.

Appendix C

Statutes and Regulations of Serampore College

June 12th, 1833

1. Article the Third of the Charter granted by his Danish Majesty, having authorised the first Council of Serampore College in their lifetime to nominate under their hand and seal such other persons for colleagues or successors as may to them appear most proper, so that the Council shall always consist of at least three persons, their successors in the Council shall be competent in like manner to nominate in their lifetime, under their separate hand and seal, such person or persons as they may deem most proper to fill vacancies then existing or which may occur on their demise; members thus nominated and chosen shall succeed to the Council in order of their nomination.

2. It being fixed in the Charter that the

Council must consist of the Master or President and at least two, but no more than four members, and that on the demise of the Master no act shall be done until another be elected, the Master and Council for the time being shall appoint the next Master under their separate hand and seal. If on the demise of a Master no one be found thus appointed under the hand and seal of a majority of the Council, the Senior Member of the Council shall succeed as Master.

3. The Charter having given the casting vote to the Master, in all cases when the votes are equal the casting vote shall lie with the Master, and if there be no Master, it shall lie with the Senior Member of the Council.

4. Learning and piety being peculiar to no denomination of Christians, one member of the Council may at all times be of any other denomination besides the Baptist, to preserve the original design of the Institution; however, if on the election of a Master a number of the Council be equally divided, that part which is entirely of the Baptist denomination shall have the casting vote, whether it includes the Master or not.

5. The management of the College, including its revenues and property, the choice of professors and Tutors, the admission of Students, the appointment of all functionaries and

servants, and the general order and government of the College, shall ever be vested in the Master and the Council. The Master shall see that the Statutes and Regulations of the Council be duly carried into effect, and take order for the good government of the College in all things. His signature is necessary to the validity of all deeds, instruments, documents and proceedings.

6. "The first Council and their successors for ever" being authorised by the Charter "to confer such degrees of rank and honour as shall encourage learning" in the same manner as other Colleges and Universities, they shall from time to time confer degrees in such branches of knowledge and Science as may be studied there, in the same manner as the Universities in Denmark, Germany and Great Britain. In doing this the Master and Council shall *ad libitum* call in the aid of any or all the Professors of Serampore College. All such degrees shall be perfectly free of expense to the person on whom they may be conferred, whether he be in India, Europe or America.

7. No oaths shall be administered in Serampore College, either to the Members of Council, the Professors and Tutors, or the Students. In all cases, a solemn promise, duly recorded and signed by the party, shall be accepted instead of an oath.

8. Marriage shall be no bar to any office or situation in Serampore College, from that of the Master to that of the lowest student.

9. The salaries of the Professors and Tutors in Serampore College shall be appointed, and the means of support for all functionaries, students, and servants be regulated by the Council in such manner as shall best promote the objects of the Institution.

10. It is intended that neither the Master nor any member of the council in general shall receive any salary. But any Master who may not previously reside in the College shall have a residence there free of rent for himself and his family. And if the Council shall elect any one in Europe or in America, whom they deem eminent for learning and piety, a Member of the Council, with a view to choosing him Master, should they on trial deem him worthy, the Council shall be competent to appoint him such salary as they may deem necessary, not exceeding, however, the highest given to a Professor.

11. As the founders of the College deem the belief of Christ's Divinity and Atonement essential to vital Christianity, the promotion of which is the grand object of this Institution, no one shall be eligible to the College Council or to any Professorship who is known to oppose these doctrines, and should any one of the

Professors or any member of the Council unhappily so change his views after his election as to oppose these fundamental doctrines of Christianity, on this being clearly and decidedly proved from his teaching or his writings, he shall vacate the office he previously held. But every proceeding of this nature on the part of the College Council shall be published to the Christian world, with the proofs on which it may rest, as an Appendix to the succeeding Report.

12. Members of the Council are eligible from among the Professors of the College, or from among any in India, Europe, or America whom the College Council may deem suitable in point of learning, piety, and talent.

13. Students are admissible at the discretion of the Council from any body of Christians, whether Protestant, Roman Catholic, the Greek, or the Armenian Church; and for the purposes of study, from the Mussulman and Hindu youth, whose habits forbid their living in the College. No caste, colour, or country shall bar any man from admission into Serampore College.

14. Expulsion shall be awarded in cases of open immorality, incorrigible idleness, neglect of the College Statutes and regulations, or repeated disobedience to the officers of the College.

15. Any person in India, Europe, or America shall be at liberty to found any Professorship, or to attach to Serampore College any annual exhibition or prize for the encouragement of learning in the same manner as in the Universities of Great Britain, regulating such endowment according to their own will; and it shall be the duty of the College Council to carry such benefactions into effect in strict consonance with the will of the donors as far as shall be consistent with the Statutes of the College.

16. It shall be lawful for the first Council of the College or their successors to make and rescind any bye-laws whatever, provided they be not contrary to these Statutes.

17. The Charter having declared that the number of the Professors and students in Serampore remains unlimited, they shall be left thus unlimited, the number to be regulated only by the gracious providence of God and the generosity of the public in India, Europe and America.

Appendix D

Article VI, Clause 2, of the Treaty of Purchase, Transferring Serampore to the British Government

The rights and immunities granted to the Serampore College by Royal Charter of date, 23rd February, 1827, shall not be interfered with, but continue in force in the same manner as if they had been obtained by a Charter from the British government, subject to the general law of British India.

Bibliography

ALLAN, HAIG DODWELL. *The Cambridge Shorter History of India*. Cambridge: 1934.

ALLEN, E. and McLURE, EDMUND. *Two Hundred Years, the History of the S.P.C.K. 1698-1898*. London: 1898.

ANDERSON, COURTNEY. *To The Golden Shore*. Boston: Little, Brown & Co., 1956.

ANDERSON, HUGH. *The Life and Letters of Christopher Anderson*. Edinburgh: 1854.

ANDREW, A. *Indian Problems*. Madras: 1905.

ANDREWS, C. F. *The Renaissance in India*. Edinburgh: 1902.

BADLEY, B. H. *Indian Missionary Directory*. Lucknow: 1876.

BATEMAN, JOSIAH. *Life of the right Rev. Daniel Wilson*. 2nd ed. London: 1861.

BEACH, HARLAN P. *Geography and Atlas of Protestant Missions*. New York: Student Volunteer Movement, 1902.

BEACH, HARLAN P. and FAHS, CHARLES H. *World Missionary Atlas*. London: 1925.

BOUSTEAD, GUY. *The Lone Monarch* (Geo. III).

BUCHANAN, CLAUDIUS. *Christian Researches in India*. London: 1840.

CAREY, EUSTACE. *Memoir of Carey*. London: 1836.

CAREY, EUSTACE. *Supplement to the Vindication of the Calcutta Baptist Missionaries*. London: 1831.

CAREY, S. PEARCE. *William Carey*. London: Hodder & Stoughton, Ltd.

CHOULER and SMITH. *The Origin and History of Missions*. New York: 1851.

CHRISTLIEB. *The Foreign Missions of Protestantism*. London: 1881.

CLARKE, W. K. L. *A History of the S.P.C.K.* London: Society for Promoting Christian Knowledge, 1959.

CLARKE, WM. NEWTON. *A Study of Christian Missions*. London: 1900.

CLARKSON, WILLIAM. *Christ and Missions*. London: 1858.

CORREIA, ALFONSO JOHN. *Jesuit Letters and Indian History*. Bombay: 1955.

COX, F. A. *History of the Baptist Missionary Society*. 2 vols. London: 1842.

CREIGHTON, LOUISE. *Missions, Their Rise and Development*. London.

CROIL, JAMES. *The Missionary Problem*. Toronto: 1883.

CUST, R. H. *Evangelization of the Non-Christian World*. London: 1894.

DAKIN, ARTHUR. *William Carey*. London.

DAS, S. *William Carey* (Bengali). Calcutta.

DATTA, S. K. *The Desire of India*. Edinburgh: 1908.

DAY, LAL BEHARI. *Recollections of Alexander Duff, D.D.* London: 1879.

DE, SUSIL KUMAR. *History of the Bengali Language and Literature.*

DENNIS, JAMES S. *Foreign Missions after a Century.* Edinburgh: 1894.

DENNIS, JAMES S. *Christian Missions and Social Progress.* 3 vols. New York: 1897.

DUFF, ALEXANDER. *India and India Missions.* Edinburgh: 1834.

EDDY, GEORGE SHERWOOD. *The New Era in Asia.* Edinburgh: 1914.

ELLIS, HARRIETT W. *Our Eastern Sisters.* London: 1886.

ELLIS, WILLIAM. *History of the London Missionary Society.* London: 1844.

ELLIS, WILLIAM T. *Men and Missions.* London: 1909.

FENWICK, JOHN. *Biographical Sketch of Joshua Marshman.* Newcastle: 1843.

FINDLAY, G. G. and HOLDSWORTH, E. E. *The History of the Wesleyan Methodist Missionary Society.* 5 vols. London: 1921.

FLEMING, D. J. *Schools with a Message in India.* London: 1921.

FRERE, SIR BARTLE. *Indian Missions.* 1874.

GOGERLY, GEORGE. *The Pioneer: A Narrative of facts connected with early Christian Missions in Bengal.* London: 1871.

GRANT, A. *Missions: Bampton Lectures.* London: 1845.

GREEN, S. G. *The Story of the Religious Tract Society*. London: 1899.

HAMPDEN, JOHN. *An Eighteenth Century Journal*. 1774-1776.

HERVEY, G. E. *The Story of Baptist Missions*. St. Louis: 1885.

HIRTZEL, ARTHUR. *The Church, the Empire, and the World*. New York: 1919.

HOBY, JAMES. *Memoir of William Yates, D.D.* London: 1847.

HOLE, CHARLES. *The Early History of the Church Missionary Society*. London: 1896.

HOLLAND, W. E. S. *The Indian Outlook*. London: 1926.

HOOLE, ELIJAH. *The Year-Book of Missions*. London: 1926.

HORNE, C. S. *The Story of the London Missionary Society*. London: 1896.

HOUGH, JAMES. *The Missionary Vade Mecum*. London: 1832.

HUIE, JAMES A. *History of Christian Missions*. Edinburgh: 1842.

HUME, ROBERT A. *Missions from the Modern View*. New York: Fleming H. Revell & Co., 1905.

HUNTER, ROBERT. *History of the Missions of the Free Church of Scotland*. London: 1873.

INGHAM, KENNETH. *Reformers in India*. Cambridge: Cambridge University Press, 1956.

JACKSON, JOHN. *Lepers*. London: 1906.

JOHNSTON, J. *Analysis of the Report of the Indian Education Commission*. London: 1884.

KAYE, JOHN WM. *Christianity in India*. London: 1859.

LATOURETTE, K. S. *A History of the Expansion of Christianity*. Vol. III. London: Eyre & Spottiswoode, Ltd., 1940.

LAWRENCE, E. A. *Modern Missions in the East*. New York: 1894.

LE BAS, CHARLES. *Life of Dr. Middleton*. 2 vols. London: 1883.

LEWIS, C. B. *Life of John Thomas*.

LONGRIDGE, GEORGE. *A History of the Oxford Mission to Calcutta*. London: 1900.

LOVETT, RICHARD. *History of the London Missionary Society, 1795-1895*. 2 vols. London: 1899.

LOWE, JOHN. *Medical Missions*. London: 1886.

LUCAS, BERNARD. *The Empire of Christ*. London: 1909.

LUSHINGTON, CHARLES. *The History of the Religious, Benevolent, and Charitable Institutions founded by the British in Calcutta*. Calcutta: 1824.

McFAYDEN, J. F. *The Missionary Idea in Life and Religion*. Edinburgh: 1926.

MACKICHAN, D. *The Missionary Ideal in the Scottish Churches*. London: 1927.

MACNICOL, NICOL. *The Making of Modern India*. London: 1924.

MANUEL, D. G. *A Gladdening River*. London: 1914.

MARSHMAN, J. C. *The History of the Serampore Mission*. Serampore: 1852.

MARSHMAN, JOHN CLARK. *The Life and Times of Carey, Marshman and Ward.* 2 vols. London: 1859.

MARSHMAN, J. C. *The Life and Labours of Carey, Marshman and Ward.* New York: 1867.

MARSHMAN, JOSHUA. *Propagation of Christianity.*

MARTYN, HENRY. *Journals and Letters.* 2 vols. London: 1838.

MAYHEW, ARTHUR. *Christianity and the Government of India.*

MIDDLEBROOK, J. B. *William Carey.* London: 1961.

MOORSHEAD, R. FLETCHER. *The Appeal of Medical Missions.* Edinburgh: 1913.

MORRIS, HENRY. *The Life of Charles Grant.* London: 1904.

MORRISON, J. H. *The Scottish Churches' Work Abroad.* Edinburgh: 1927.

MORRISON, J. H. *William Carey, Cobbler and Pioneer.* London: Hodder and Stoughton, Ltd.

MOSCROP, THOMAS. *The Kingdom without Frontiers.* London: 1910.

MOTT, JOHN R. *Strategic Points in the World's Conquest.* New York: 1897.

MULLENS, JOSEPH. *London and Calcutta.* London: 1869.

MULLENS, JOSEPH. *Brief Memorials of the Rev. A. F. Lacroic.* London: 1862.

MURDOCH, JOHN. *Education as a Missionary Agency in India.* Madras: 1872.

MYERS, J. B. *William Carey.* London: S. W. Partridge & Co., 1887.

NOEL, BAPTIST. *England and India*. London: 1859.

OGILVIE, J. H. *An Indian Pilgrimage*. 2nd Ed.; Edinburgh: 1922.

OLCOTT, MASON. *Village Schools in India*. Calcutta: 1926.

OUSSOREN, AALBERTINUS H. *William Carey*. Leiden: 1945.

PASCOE, C. F. *Two Hundred Years of the S.P.G.* London: 1901.

PAYNE, ERNEST. *Growth of the World Church*. London: Edinburgh House Press, 1955.

PIERSON, ARTHUR T. *The Divine Enterprise of Missions*. London: 1892.

PIERSON, ARTHUR T. *The Miracles of Missions*. New York: 1891.

PIERSON, ARTHUR T. *The New Acts of the Apostles*. London: 1894.

PLATH, CARL H. C. *The Subject of Missions*. Edinburgh: 1873.

PLATTNER, FELIX. *Christian India*. New York: Vanguard Press, Inc., 1957.

RICHTER, JULIUS. *A History of Missions in India*. Edinburgh: 1908.

RITSON, JOHN H. *Christian Literature in the Mission Field*. Edinburgh: 1910.

ROBERTS, JOSEPH. *Caste Opposed to Christianity*. 2nd ed. London: 1847.

ROBINSON, C. H. *History of Christian Missions*. Edinburgh: 1915.

ROBINSON, C. H. *The Interpretation of the Character of Christ to Non-Christian Races*. London: 1910.

Robinson, C. K. *Missions Urged Upon the State*. Cambridge: 1853.

Rutnam, S. C. K. *An Oriental Study of Foreign Missions*. London: 1920.

Ryland, John. *Memoirs of Fuller*.

St. Clair-Tisdall, W. *India*. London: 1901.

Sargent, J. *Life of Rev. T. T. Thomason*. 2nd ed. London: 1834.

Scudder, W. W. *Nineteen Centuries of Missions*. Edinburgh: 1901.

Sherring, M. A. *The History of Protestant Missions in India*. London: 1875.

Silen, E. *William Carey*. Stockholm: 1934.

Singh, Behari Lal. *History of Native Female Education in Calcutta*. 2nd ed. Calcutta: 1858.

Slater, T. E. *The Philosophy of Missions*. London: 1882.

Smith, George. *Life of William Carey*. 2nd ed. London: John Murray, 1887.

Smith, George. *Bishop Heber*. London: 1895.

Smith, George. *The Conversion of India*. London: 1893.

Smith, George. *Short History of Christian Missions*. Edinburgh: 1904.

Smith, George. *The Life of Alexander Duff, D.D., LL.D.*

Smith, Vincent A. *The Oxford History of India*. Oxford: 1923.

Smith, William S. *Obstacles to Missionary Success among the Heathen*. London: 1868.

Stennett. *Life of Ward*.

STEWART, W. (ed.). *The Story of Serampore and Its College.*

STOCK, EUGENE. *The History of the Church Missionary Society.* 4 vols. London: 1899, 1916.

STOCK, EUGENE. *A Short Handbook of Missions.* London: 1904.

STORROW, EDWARD. *India and Christian Missions.* London: 1859.

STORROW, EDWARD. *Our Indian Sisters.* London: 1890.

TISSERANT, EUGENE. *Eastern Christianity in India.* Westminster: 1957.

TWEEDIE, W. K. *Life of the Rev. J. MacDonald of Calcutta.* Edinburgh: 1849.

UNDERHILL, EDWARD B. *Life of Rev. John Wenger, D.D.* London: 1886.

URQUHART, MARGARET M. *Women of Bengal.* 2nd ed. London: 1926.

WALKER, F. DEAVILLE. *William Carey, Missionary Pioneer and Statesman.* London: Student Christian Movement, 1926.

WARD, F. *India and the Hindoos.* Glasgow: 1853.

WARD, W. *Description of the Religious Manners and Customs of the Hindoos.* 3 vols. Serampore: 1808.

WARNECK, GUSTAV. *A History of Protestant Missions.* Edinburgh: 1901.

WEIR, R. W. *Foreign Missions of the Church of Scotland.* Edinburgh: 1900.

WEITBRECHT, MRS. *The Women of India and Christian Work in the Zenana.* London: 1875.

WEITBRECHT, MRS. *Female Missionaries in India.* London: 1843.

WEITBRECHT, MRS. *Missionary sketches in North India.* London: 1858.

WEITBRECHT, J. J. *Protestant Missions in Bengal.* London: 1844.

WENGER, E. S. *The Story of the Lall Bazar Baptist Church.* Calcutta: 1908.

WHERRY, E. M. *Islam and Christianity in India and Far East.* New York: 1907.

WILKINSON, M. *Sketches of Christianity in North India.* London: 1844.

WILLIAMS, BASIL. *The Whig Supremacy, 1714-1760. (Oxford History of England.)*

WILLIAMS, LEIGHTON and MORWAY. *Serampore Letters.* London: 1892.

WILSON, R. S. *The Indirect Effects of Christian Missions in India.* London: 1929.

WISHARD, LUTHER D. *A New Programme of Missions.* New York: 1895.

WOODWARD. *The Age of Reform 1815-1870. (Oxford History of England.)*

WYLIE, M. *Bengal as a Field of Missions.* London: 1854.

YATES, WM. *Memoirs of W. H. Pearce.* Abridged by Hoby. London: 1847.

YOUNG, ROBERT. *Modern Missions.* London: 1883.

REPORTS AND CONFERENCES

Accounts, Periodical—Relative to the B.M.S.

vols. I-X dealing with years 1792-1844. London.

Accounts, Periodical—Of the Serampore Mission 1827-28, Edinburgh, 1828.

Centenary of the Baptist Missionary Society, 1792-1892.

Centenary of the L.M.S.—London, 1895.

Chronicle, Quarterly, of Transactions of the L.M.S., 1815-19, London, 1821.

Conference of Bengal Missionaries, 1855.

India and Oxford, 50 years of the Oxford Mission to Calcutta. London.

Indian Educational Policy, (Resolution issued by Governor-General in Council on March 11, 1904). Calcutta, 1904.

Jubilee Volume of the C.M.S., 1848-49, London, 1849.

Our Church's Work in India (Story of the U. F. Church of Scotland), Edinburgh.

Records, *Classified Digest of the Records of the S. P. G. in Foreign Parts, 1701-1892,* 2nd ed. London, 1893.

Report, *Of the Centenary Conference of Protestant Missions of the World,* London, 1888.

Report, *One Hundred Years of the C.M.S.,* London, 1899.

Report, *Religious Awakening at Krishnagar,* London, 1840.

Report, *To the General Assembly of the Church of Scotland, Foreign Missions Committee,* for the years 1836-1930.

Reports, Annual, Church Missionary Society,
    1816 to 1834.
Reports, Annual, London Missionary Society,
    1800-1834.
Reports, Serampore College, 1819-1827.
*Reports, Annual, Society for the Propagation of
    the Gospel,* for the years 1825-1919.
Serampore Circular Letters. 3 vols. 1811-1813,
    1814-1816, 1817-1819.

NEWSPAPERS AND MAGAZINES

Dig Darshan, Bengali monthly magazine, Seram-
    pore, 1818, 1819, 1820.
Friend of India, Serampore, (weekly).
Friend of India, Serampore, (monthly) Nos. I-IX.
Friend of India, Serampore, (quarterly) Nos. 2-4.
*The Home and Foreign Missionary Record of the
    Church of Scotland,* 1839 to 1890.
Missionary Chronicle, 1826 to 1833.
Missionary Herald, Baptist Missionary Society,
    1819 to 1834.
Samachar Durpun, Bengali weekly newspaper,
    Serampore, 1831 to 1834.

LETTERS AND MANUSCRIPTS

Miscellaneous Letters of Carey, Marshman, Ward,
Fuller, Ryland, and Brunsdon in London, Bristol,
and Northampton.

Manuscript Journal of Carey, June 13, 1793 to
October 2, 1795.

Manuscript Journal of Ward, May 1799 to October 1811.

Correspondence of Mr. Joseph Gutteridge of Camberwell on affairs of the B.M.S., 1812 to 1831.

Missionary Biographies by E. S. Wenger, 4 volumes in manuscript form with notes on every B.M.S. missionary from 1792 to 1911. (This is in the Serampore Library.)

PAMPHLETS

Supplement to the Vindication of the Calcutta Baptist Missionaries occasioned by Dr. Carey's "Thirty-Two Letters," Dr. Marshman's "Reply to the Rev. John Dyer" and Mr. John Marshman's "Review" by Eustace Carey. London, 1831.

A letter to the President of the Board of Control on the Propagation of Christianity in India. London, 1807.

A letter to the Chairman of the East India Company on the danger of interfering in the religious opinions of the natives of India by Thomas Twining. London, 1807.

An address to the Chairman of the East India Company occasioned by Mr. Twining's letter to that gentleman on the danger of interfering in the religious opinions of the natives of India by the Rev. John Owen. London, 1807.

Two letters to the Proprietors of East India Stock occasioned by Mr. Twining's late letter to the Chairman and some anonymous observations on the present state of India urging the suppression of the Scriptures and the recall of the missionaries from that country. London, 1807.

A few cursory remarks on Mr. Twining's letter to the Chairman by a member of the British and Foreign Bible Society. London, 1807.

Observations on the present state of the East India Company by John Scott Waring. London, 1807.

Observations on the present state of the East India Company with prefatory remarks on the alarming intelligence lately received from Madras as to the general disaffection prevailing amongst the natives of every rank from an opinion that it is the intention of the British Government to compel them to embrace Christianity. London, 1807.

A letter to the Rev. John Owen in reply to the brief strictures by Major Scott Waring. London, 1808.

A letter to John Scott Waring with strictures on his illiberal and unjust conduct towards the missionaries in India. London, 1808.

Christianity in India: An Essay on the duty, means and consequences of introducing the Christian Religion among the native inhabitants of the British dominions in the East by J. Cunningham. London, 1808.

An apology for the late Christian Missions to India by Andrew Fuller. London, 1808.

Considerations on the Practicability, Policy and Obligations of communicating to the natives of India the knowledge of Christianity with observations on the "Prefatory Remarks" to a pamphlet published by Major Scott Waring by a late resident in Bengal. London, 1808.

The dangers of British India from French invasion and missionary establishments by a late resident at Bhagulpore. London, 1808.

Vindication of the Hindoos from the Aspersions of the Reverend Claudius Buchanan, M.A., with a refutation of the arguments exhibited in his memoir on the expediency of an ecclesiastical establishment for British India and the ultimate civilization of the natives by their conversion to Christianity by a Bengal Officer. London, 1808.

Debates at the East India House during the negotiations for a renewal of the East India Company's charter in the year 1813 by an impartial reporter. Two volumes. London, 1813.

Observations on the State of Society among the Asiatic subjects of Great Britain particularly with respect to morals and on the means of improving it by Charles Grant. 1792.

A reply to a letter addressed to John Scott Waring by Major Scott Waring. London, 1808.

Christianity in India: letters between Laicus and an East India proprietor as they appeared in the *Times* newspaper in the months of August, September, and October, 1813. London.

Letters on the Serampore Controversy addressed to the Rev. Christopher Anderson occasioned by Postscript dated Edinburgh 26th November, 1830, affixed to the "Reply" of the Rev. Dr. Marshman by Joseph Ivimey. London, 1831.

Reply of Mr. J. C. Marshman to the attack of Mr. Buckingham on the Serampore Missionaries. London, 1826.

Reply of the Serampore missionaries to the attack made on them in No. 111 of the *Oriental* magazine. Serampore, 1824.

Statement relative to Serampore supplementary to a "Brief Memoir" by J. Marshman, D.D. London, 1828.

Review of two pamphlets by the Rev. John Dyer and the Rev. E. Carey and W. Yates in 12 letters to the Rev. John Foster by J. C. Marshman. London, 1830.

Two letters to the Committee of the B.M.S. on their disputes with the Serampore Brethren by an old subscriber to the Baptist Mission. London, 1829.

Letters from the Rev. Dr. Carey relative to certain statements contained in three pamphlets lately published by the Rev. John Dyer, Secre-

tary to the B.M.S., W. Johns, M.D. and the Rev.
E. Carey and W. Yates. London, 1828.

An apology for promoting Christianity in India
by the Rev. Claudius Buchanan, D.D. London,
1813.